One Way Out

To Terri,
So glad to have become acquainted with you and Steve.
May God bless and keep you!
Buddy

BUDDY DAVIS

ISBN 978-1-63961-279-6 (paperback)
ISBN 978-1-63961-280-2 (digital)

Christian Faith Publishing
832 Park Avenue
Meadville, PA 16335
www.christianfaithpublishing.com

Printed in the United States of America

INTRODUCTION

This book is about the life and times of a boy named Buddy, who grew up in the '70s. It is a true storytelling about all the mistakes he made trying to find his place in this world. After moving out of his parents' house to share an apartment with friends at the age of seventeen and also losing his father the same year, his mom moved in with a sister because she was getting up in years and the neighborhood was getting more and more unsafe. This made Buddy realize that his childhood home, his safety net, was no longer there for him to go back to. He was on his own. From that point on, he decided that partying and being with friends would be his life. After years of drinking, failed relationships, and nearly dying three times, he would find a way, slowly but surely, to get his life back on track.

Thank you, Mom, for always praying for me!

CHAPTER 1

It was a hot, very humid day in Houston, Texas, a nice day as I recall. The thing about it was I don't recall many Sundays back in those days. You've heard how Sunday should be a day of rest? Well, back in those days, I really didn't have much choice. I was usually too hung over from partying and drinking Friday and Saturday nights to do anything else but rest.

This particular Sunday, however, my head was clear for once. Yes, I'd been out the night before and had a couple of beers, but only a couple. Now I was on my way to Sam Houston Hospital, where I was to have a severely torn cartilage in my left knee removed the next day. I wasn't really looking forward to that, mind you, but like it is with most unpleasant things in life, I was looking forward to having it behind me.

My friend Roy was driving me to the hospital on that uncertain afternoon; I think that Roy knew at that point I certainly knew that my marriage to Sally was behind me. He was trying hard not to though at that point he was still pretending things were salvageable as I had been doing for so long. I'd been staying with Roy and his wife, Connie, for the past couple of nights. Sally and I had had another of our blowups—this one, of all things, about my upcoming surgery.

The last thing Sally had said to me was "Go ahead and have your damn operation, but don't bother coming back here!"

I fired back at her: "Don't worry, bitch, I won't."

So Roy and Connie had taken me in like a homeless puppy the day before.

Saturday afternoon, Roy had been determined to cheer me up, so he said to me, "Buddy, let's get the hell out of here and go have some fun."

So we had gotten ourselves cleaned up—Roy, Connie, and me—and headed on down the road to Pasadena, Texas, and Gilley's club. It was my first time there. It was a very big place and very interesting. I wasn't much of a cowboy, but I noticed there were a lot of pretty women.

Looking back on that night, I'm sure that I wasn't very good company. Janie Frickie was the featured artist that night. She sang those country and Western songs of hers like an angel as I recall. It was all sort of lost on me though; I was preoccupied with the surgery that was in front of me and the marriage that seemed almost certainly behind me at that point, and my knee was starting to hurt from all the walking we had to do. I suppose that is why I didn't try to do any dancing that night, which I normally loved to do. For that matter, the beer wasn't flowing as smoothly as it usually does. I did my best not to think about my problems, but you know what that's like—the more you try to ignore them, the more they crowd in on you. The surgery, my all but over marriage, and the two-year-old daughter I was leaving behind me—all those things were spinning around in my head like leaves in a whirlpool. Believe me, it seemed like that night lasted forever.

Finally, about midnight, Connie looked over at Roy and said, "Come on, honey, let's get out of here. I'm getting tired."

Roy looked over at me, of all people, and asked, "Are you ready to go?"

My brilliant retort was, "Hell no, I'm waiting for the last call!"

Luckily, however, no one believed me, and we started making our way slowly, more walking, out into the still sweltering Texas night. We were out in the parking lot now, and I couldn't help but notice all of the vehicles parked there.

Damn, what an assortment of pickup trucks, I thought. And nearly every one of them had the bumper sticker given out by the local radio station KIKK. The stickers either said I'M PROUD TO BE A KIKKER or KIKKUP TRUCK. I didn't think we had to worry about getting a sticker because we came in a 1976 Ford LTD, not a truck.

All of a sudden, I heard Roy throwing a fit. Apparently, someone had also put a sticker on his car—well, actually Connie's car. Either way, he wasn't really happy about it.

He kneeled down to try and rip it off, but Connie stopped him. "Just leave it, and we'll worry about it tomorrow." Later I found out that she actually liked it.

Finally, we were headed home, Connie driving, Roy up on the front seat beside her, and me sort of sprawled out across the backseat. This was before so much was made about the designated driver, but Connie didn't drink—ever—so that made for a really nice setup for Roy. Just as we pulled out into traffic, Roy reached into the cooler he had brought and handed me a cold can of Schlitz for the drive home; and forty-five minutes later, when we got back to their apartment, he handed me another.

"Hell, Buddy," he said. "I mean, why not? It's the last night before you go into the hospital after all. You mark my words now— you'll go into that hospital and you'll get that bum knee all fixed up and then you'll go right back home and get your marriage fixed up. It'll work out, you wait and see."

"Sure, man," I replied. "Whatever you say."

At this point, I wasn't exactly sure I wanted my marriage to be fixed. You see, there was just no more love to be lost between Sally and me. There never had been that much to start with, for that matter. The only real bond that we had left was our baby girl. Sally and I had fought drunk, we had fought sober, we fought fair, and we fought unfairly. We had fought just about every hour of the day and night. You name it—and Sally and I fought about it. I hate to admit it, but a couple of times I came very close to striking her; and if it was bad for us, what was it doing to this little two-year-old baby? At that tender age, maybe she just thought it was normal. What a horrible thought.

* * * * *

"Buddy?"

I shook myself back to reality. Roy's truck had stopped, and he was sort of leaning across the front seat, grinning at me.

"We're here, man, at the hospital." He paused for a moment. "Where in the hell were you just now? You were a million miles away."

"No, not quite a million," I said. "So that's the hospital, huh? Nice-looking place, eh, Roy?"

I think I was just trying to convince myself. I really didn't want to get out of the truck and go in there, but I knew, of course, I had to.

"Nice enough for a hospital, I guess," Roy said. "You know me, Buddy, I never did like hospitals, probably never will."

"Never?" I asked.

"No, never," grinning at me now as he pulled into a parking spot. "If the good Lord wanted me to like hospitals, he would have made me a doctor instead of a tile setter."

Hmm, the good Lord, huh. I hadn't thought about the good Lord for a while. I wonder if he's thinking about me? I hoped so. Right now I'm gonna need all the help I can get!

I had to hand it to Roy—he was really good to me that day. He did not like hospitals, and I knew that he didn't, but he didn't just dump me out at the front door; he stayed with me until I was settled in. We went in and got all the paperwork filled out, and then he walked beside me while the orderly rolled me up to my room. Then after the orderly left, he played with the remote control of the TV, checking out the stations.

"What! No cable?" he said. He set the remote down on the bed then clapped me on the shoulder and said, "Well, Buddy, I guess I better be getting on down the road. I just know that things are gonna work out for you…the operation and, well, you know. Call me if you need anything, brother. I mean that!" He gave a little wave of his hand, and out the door he went.

"Hey, Roy," I yelled. "Thanks for everything, man!"

And then he was gone, and there I sat alone—nobody to talk to, no place to go.

"I wonder if they have room service in this resort," I muttered to myself as I stood up and hobbled over to the window. I pulled back the curtains to let the sunshine in. It was a beautifully clear afternoon, but my room was on the wrong side of the hospital to catch the afternoon sun. However, that wasn't too bad of a view I had of the parking lot down below. I could sit and watch the cars go by and the people walking around, talking about whatever. My leg was really beginning to hurt me now. That had been a dumb trick going out the night before and doing all that walking. Of course, that has been Roy's idea, not mine; and after all, he had really just been trying to get my mind off my problems. I hobbled back to the bed and lay down. I was in a semiprivate room, but I had it all to myself for the present at least. I flipped quickly through the television channels again; there was nothing on that I wanted to see anyway. So I just sort of lay there for a while, listening to the muffled noises from the hall.

The occasional distant sound of people talking, footsteps going up and down, a modulated voice over the PA system, a soft bell ringing somewhere. Suddenly it dawned on me that I was at peace with myself—for the first time in a long time. This was really nice, relaxing. That's what it was—relaxing—and gradually I found myself making plans for the time when I would have the surgery behind me. Not quite as starry-eyed as the scenario that Roy had spun for me the night before, mind you, but optimistic nonetheless. First, I get my knee fixed up, I thought. That's number one, that's tomorrow. Then I get out of here, and I get a place of my own. Yes, that's the ticket. I'll get a place that's all mine, nobody else to worry about, nobody to bug me or to fight with—just me!

And then, as it always seems to do eventually, reality sets in. Just me? No way. What about that little baby girl? Sally and I would be divorced, that was a certainty. There was no way in the world that we could ever get that relationship back into shape. The sad truth was we never really had a strong relationship. But what about this little kid who had taken a piece of my heart, who was in a real sense of a part of me. Thinking about her and what we were doing to her made me ache with a hurting that completely eclipsed the hurting in my knee. Tomorrow my knee would be fixed, and eventually, that pain would go away. But this hurt that I was feeling over my kid was sharper and deeper than any physical pain could ever be. And when would that pain end? I didn't know then, but now I know—it never ends.

However, had I gotten myself into such a mess? I wondered. One thing was for sure, if my father had been living, I wouldn't be in this fix. For that matter, I probably wouldn't even be in Texas. Dad had been gifted with a surefire way of making a person see the error of his ways. It hadn't had much to do with subtle arguments or philosophy, but it had surely been effective nonetheless.

Lying there in my hospital bed whiling away that Sunday afternoon, I thought back to a time—it must have been when I was in the seventh grade. Yes, I was in the seventh grade, and the girl in this case—her name was Alice I remember—had been in the eighth grade. By that time in my life, I had had a few crushes on cute girls but never dated any. A female friend of mine told me that her friend thought I was cute! So, of course, after hearing this, I had to meet this young lady. We hung out before and after school sometimes and talked about things, but nothing too serious. There was a time when we passed notes back and forth, which was the cool thing to do in junior high school.

Well anyway, as things progressed, I got her phone number and called her up one night and asked her if she wanted to meet me at the Little League field to watch a game. This was a really big step for me because in actuality, I had just asked a girl out on a date! She agreed. We set a time to meet, and now the date was on. Now this Little League field that I am speaking of was a good eight miles from my house. I started thinking even with a good knee at that time of my life, it was a long way to walk. My bicycle was broken down, and I figured I would look like a dork pulling up for my first romantic evening. I had no other way to get there. Then I thought I'll just ask my dad if he could drive me over there. Besides that, I didn't really have enough time to walk and be on time.

My dad was sitting on the front porch, not doing anything, so I went out all innocent-like and asked him if he could give me a ride.

"A ride?" he asked. "Where do you want a ride to?" He looked at me suspiciously.

"To the Little League field," I answered.

"Why are you going over there?" he asked.

"Why does anybody go over there?" I replied testily.

"To watch a game!"

What is this—twenty questions I counted. I hadn't really intended to tell him about Alice, but I could see now that I would have to.

"Okay, I'm going to meet a girl there. Her name is Alice, and we're going to watch the game together. Big deal!"

Dad nodded. "I thought it was something like that. The way you're going, you're going to be married with six kids by the time you're twenty!"

Well, I really knew better than to do what I did next, but his saying this made me mad. I stood there and looked him straight in the eye and barked back at him. "Well if I do, it's my damn business and none of yours!"

The next thing I knew, I was lying on the dining room floor with an aching jaw. Now when you're standing on the porch in my old house, you have to go through the living room to get to the dining room. It's still a mystery to me how I did that without my knowing about it, but it might have had something to do with that fist I saw approaching just after I made my smart-aleck reply. Needless to say, my dad didn't take me anywhere that day—at least not to the ballpark.

Yes, if my dad had lived a little longer, I might not have been in this mess; but he had died at age sixty-five with emphysema, the result, at least partially, of all those unfiltered Camel cigarettes he had smoked for about fifty years. I was eighteen years old when my father died, and I guess the good news was that he always said he wanted to live to see me raised. Was I raised? You're probably not raised when you do as many stupid things as I did in those years.

Lying there in that hospital bed feeling more and more sorry for myself, I found myself thinking, *Face it, man...your dad can't help you now. You're going to have to face this one on your own.* And I found myself missing him more than I ever had before. See, Dad might have been a little rough around the edges—well, maybe a lot rough around the edges—but he was basically a good man, and in his own way we knew that he loved us.

Damn! My knee was really hurting me now. I was glad that I would be having the surgery tomorrow; hopefully, that would be the end of my knee problems. If only all the rest of my problems could be so easily managed. I flirted with the idea of calling the nurse and getting something for the pain, but then I decided to tough it out. What would the old gang back in Gulfport, Florida, think? George, Lurch, and Dawn, and all the rest of the gang think of me wimping out from a little bit of pain. Maybe if I just lay back for a while and rested, that would help. Goodness knows I didn't have all that much else to do right now. I scrunched around a bit and settled myself as best I could then closed my eyes.

Funny I should think of my friends back in Gulfport. That was where I had met Sally. It was at a bar called "Gulfport on the Rocks." Thinking about that, I couldn't help but smile despite my pain, thinking how prophetic that bar's name had turned out to be so far as Sally and I were concerned. Our relationship was definitely on the rocks. I remembered that Dawn had been there that night. She had been a pretty big part of my life for a while back in Gulfport.

Lying there waiting for the ache in my knee to ease off, I found my mind drifting back to those days with Dawn and the wild times we had all experienced together.

CHAPTER 2

Gulfport, Florida, back in the '70s what a place that had been to party! The lifestyle of that small waterfront town of old drunks, young drunks, bars, restaurants, gift shops for the tourists, and retired people on three-wheeled bicycles. However, there was no generation gap. Some of my best drinking buddies rode those bicycles. It had been the ruin of many a young man and woman. How I wish personally that it had been the ruin of one less person. Five bars within a quarter mile and live rock and roll screaming down the boulevard on weekends and holidays. It was a paradise for both the full-time and the part-time freaks that partied on that strip, and with the beach and Boca Ciega Bay right across the street, well, what more could you ask?

The group of friends that I hung out with had long since been drinking and had, at long last, reached drinking age as well. It was almost as sure as night follows day that we'd begin drifting toward the bar and the beach scene. About the only serious rival that I had in that crowd, party wise, was my friend Lurch. Lurch stood about six feet four and weighed, say, 130 pounds dripping wet. He had a voice like a bullfrog and tattoos just about anywhere you could stick one. Lurch and I were old friends going back to the sandlot baseball days, but as we got older, we left baseball behind us and applied ourselves to more serious pursuits such as drinking, smoking pot, and chasing the girls. At one point, Lurch and I and a clean-cut college-type boy named George—more about him later—rented a house together, and I don't suppose I was closer to anyone in those days than I was to Lurch.

Lurch never had a father or at least one that he mentioned. One time I remember we were sitting around together, sort of talking about nothing—you know what I mean. Well, somehow or other, I got to talking about my dad, a man who as you may have guessed made a considerable impression on me. After a couple of well-delivered stories about Dad and me, including the one that I told you earlier, I looked over at Lurch, and there he was sitting and looking about as solemn as an undertaker at a funeral.

It seemed obvious to me that he was bored, so I said, "Hey, so much for that. I know you're not interested in hearing about me and my dad."

"No, man," he shot back quick as a flash. "No, go on, really. I get into hearing about guys and their fathers." And then a strange little smile came over his face. "I never had a father."

Something about the way he said those words and that tight little smile on his face as he said them sent a chill up my spine. I knew that he had to be hurting deep down inside. I hadn't really thought about it before, but I had never known Lurch to reveal anything personal about himself. I felt kind of bad about the hurt that I had inadvertently caused him.

Lurch sat there, silently for a moment, and so did I. Neither of us could think what to do or say next. Finally, I took a last long swing of my beer and gave a little shake of the empty can toward Lurch. "Ready for another one, man?" I said. Okay, it wasn't exactly Neil Simon's dialogue, but it was the best I could come up with at the time.

I think that he was glad to also get off the hook because he held out his empty to me and said, "Sure," in what sounded to me like a grateful tone of voice.

I dumped the empties in the trash and went to the refrigerator for replacements. At least the pause gave me a chance to think of some way to change the subject—away from what was obviously a painful one to my friend. *Hey*, I thought, gratefully, grasping at straws. *I know what to do. All I need to do is start talking about his tattoos.*

14

Tattoos were something that Lurch was always ready to talk about especially the thirty-two that were on his body. Lots of people wear chains around their wrists, but Lurch had a chain tattooed around his wrist. He once told me that his fondest ambition was to put as many tattoos on his body as he could and then fill in all around them with some sort of paisley design.

"Then when I die, there won't be any need to worry about what to dress me in. Just lay me out naked in my casket in all my glory."

Lurch had actually put on a lot of his own tattoos. He had a lot that he'd gone to tattoo parlors for as well. On one shoulder, he had the word *Dad* (the father that he'd never known) followed by the date that he had died. But the one that always spooked me was a beautiful red rose that he had on his right forearm. It had a sharp-pointed dagger through the center of it, and carefully scripted above it was the word *Mother*. But the tattoo on him that impressed me the most was the one that was on his right upper back, and that again was one of his originals. While standing in front of a bathroom mirror and holding a small mirror in his hand, he had self-inscribed:

> Don't walk behind me,
> I may not lead.
> Don't walk in front of me,
> I may not follow.
> Just walk beside me,
> And be my friend!

I'm glad that Lurch was my friend, but my oh my! We surely did raise some hell together!

CHAPTER 3

I told you that Lurch and George and I were roommates for a while. I got home from work one Friday afternoon, dog tired and dripping wet with sweat from working outside all day in the heat. About all I wanted out of life at that moment was a cold beer and a hot shower—in no particular order of preference. As I came into the house, I heard the shower running, so that limited the choices a bit. But that was all right; I could do with a cold brew. I went into the kitchen, pulling off my shirt as I went, and opened the refrigerator door. As it happened, there was no beer. George or Lurch must have finished it off. There was, however, a big beautiful pitcher of cold iced tea.

Well...hell, I thought. Any port in a storm. I was so hot and thirsty along about then that I really didn't care much about what I drank as long as it was cold, and the tea seemed to match the description. I found myself a tall glass, filled it up with tea, and slugged it down in about three seconds. Ah! That definitely hit the spot. Slipping my shirt under my arm, I headed on down the hall to my bedroom, stopping by the bathroom door, and giving a short knock to let Lurch know I was home.

"Hey, Lurch, save me some hot water, will you?"

"You got it, man." I heard his voice through the door, and almost simultaneously, I heard the water shut off.

I went back to my room and pulled off my work clothes and put on a clean pair of jeans. I was coming out of my bedroom about the same time that he was coming out of the bathroom.

"Hey, Bud," he said. "Stay out of that iced tea in the refrigerator okay," he said. It's for the party tonight."

I thought for sure he was putting me on. Tea was not the usual beverage served at our parties.

I chuckled a little bit and then said, "Sure, man. Will we also be serving crumpets with that tea?"

"Well, man," he said. "There's tea, and then there's *tea*!" The way he said that last word sent a chill of apprehension through me. Now staring at him blankly, I said, "What are you talking about?"

"Well, let's just say I made it a little more interesting with some added ingredients."

That certainly didn't make me feel any better. "What do you mean 'extra ingredients'?"

He smiled at me and said, "Blotter acid!"

I blinked. Blotter acid was LSD. I was drinking and smoking a little pot, I had never done LSD and really wasn't interested in doing any for that matter.

"How much?" I asked.

"Enough," Lurch replied.

I stared at him in disbelief. "Are you serious, man? I just drank a big glass of it!"

He just looked at me and shrugged. "Well, enjoy yourself. Just think of all the money you'll save at the liquor store."

"Hey, Lurch!" I sputtered. "You think this is funny? I don't think this is funny! Hey, man, am I gonna be okay or what?"

By this time, I was talking to his back as he headed up the pull-down ladder to the attic where he had made his bedroom. (It wasn't much, but he seemed to like it; and anyway, it seemed sort of fitting for someone known as Lurch.) Like a shot, I was after him, once again raising my concerns about what was going to happen to me.

"Hey, man, don't worry about it," he said. "Just relax and enjoy yourself." He grinned. "Look, I'm here to keep an eye on you. If anything goes wrong, I'll handle it. Just stay cool, and you'll do fine. But if you get all crazy about it, you might...freak out!"

Well, I knew I had to follow his advice. For one thing, there wasn't anything else to do. I mean the damage had been done by that time. The other thing was, well, Lurch was sort of the resident expert of our crowd on drugs, and you know by this time something of what our crowd was like. I remember sometimes people would bring pills to him because they didn't know what they were. He would look at them to see if he recognized them. He would then grind them up and shoot them up. Then he would tell the people of any sensations he was feeling.

So as it turned out, I was okay that night—but what a night! I mean so far as my experience of LSD was concerned—and that was my only experience of LSD—believe me, it was all I wanted. It wasn't at all like it was portrayed in the movies. No weird colors, no hallucinations, no Salvador Dali bending and merging. What it did to me was give me mood swings. One minute I'd be laughing and joking, and the next I'd be very serious, almost intense!

There was this girl I knew named Dawn. As a matter of fact, I always sort of had the feeling that we might end up together. Dawn sort of epitomized the crowd that I hung out with. She had been married and divorced and had three little girls as a result of her playing grown-up. Her grandmother and her sister Lora pretty much took care of the girls. Dawn had only two goals in life. The first was to find a man that could satisfy her sexually; I have no idea whether she ever achieved that one. Her second goal was, as she put it, "Get my shit together!" She was all the time saying that, and looking back, I don't know if she ever achieved that one either. Both Dawn and Lora were at the party that night. Dawn was drinking and doing a little dancing to the loud music from the speakers George had hidden in the fireplace, of all places. She was just sort of being Dawn, I guess. And there I was, swinging wildly from one mood to the other. Well, the upshot of it was I got into one of my serious moods, and of all things—damn that LSD—I asked Dawn to move in with me.

She looked at me in astonishment. "What did you just say to me, Buddy?"

I answered back quickly, "I asked you to move in with me."

"What the hell, why not?"

"Don't you think it's a good idea? You like me, right? And you're over here all the time anyway, right?"

She hesitated then answered with a little uncertainty in her voice, "I do like you, Buddy, and I guess…well…yeah, it's a good idea. Sure, I'll move in with you. Like you said, what the hell! I just can't believe that you asked me. Buddy, you just seem so serious tonight. Not like your regular self."

"Yeah," I replied. "I drank some iced tea earlier."

She looked at me as if I had said something strange; I wonder why. Then after a pause, she said tentatively, "Yeah...well, that's... that's good."

Just for something to do, I think, she planted a little kiss on my lips and continued, "Hey, I'm gonna go tell sister what just happened!" She flashed me a broad smile and gave a little shake of her head." "Oh, Buddy, you're so crazy sometimes, you know that?" Then she was off to find her sister.

As I watched her walk away, I wondered to myself, *What is so unusual about drinking iced tea?*

At about that time I was beginning to realize that Dawn really didn't care about my choice of beverages that evening. That wasn't what she was going to tell Lora about. What had I just done anyway? I better go check in with Lurch. I found him sitting all by himself off in a corner.

"Hey, man, how are you doing? How're you making it?"

"Oh, I'm okay, I guess," I said in an uncertain tone of voice. "I just asked Dawn to move in with me, and she graciously accepted."

He looked at me with the same sort of expression on his face that he might have if I had told him I had just been on board an alien spacecraft. Still staring up at me, he said, "Oh...my... God! And I thought I was keeping my eye on you. You're in worse shape than I thought!"

About that time, Dawn, Lora, and George were coming out of the kitchen and heading toward the corner where Lurch and I were. Let me tell you a little bit about George and Lora. They were a twosome, sort of like Ken and Barbie. That wasn't where the resemblance ended, for that matter. George was a clean-cut college-boy type, so you can imagine that it had taken him a little while to fit in with this crowd. There was George with his proper little haircut, and here I was with my three years' growth of mane and full beard usually wearing my hair back in a ponytail, but we ended up being pretty good friends. Once he even talked me into going cruising in his station wagon!

Lora was sort of the feminine version of George, I guess. Maybe that's why they ended up getting along so well together. In a lot of ways, she was the opposite of her sister. Lora, in contrast to Dawn, had only one goal in life, and that was to find a husband—and the quicker the better, preferably complete with a split-level mortgage, two and a half kids, and a white picket fence. So you can just imagine how good that station wagon of George's looked to her. She had made a solemn vow to remain a virgin until her wedding night, and as I remember, she damn near made it—according to George.

So here came the three of them, and was it my imagination, or was there a special little gleam in Dawn's eye as she snuggled up a little closer to me than was really necessary.

"Hey, guys," said Dawn. "No offense, but what do you say we move this party?"

"Sounds good to me," Lurch rumbled. "What do you have in mind?"

"I don't know," she said. "How about the Rocks (short for Gulfport on the Rocks)?"

Lurch gave a little shrug of his shoulders and said, "Let's do it!" Then he jumped up out of his chair and said, "Well, let's go!"

"You guys go on ahead," I mumbled. "I'm just gonna stay here."

"Oh, no, you don't," barked Lurch, reaching down and pulling me to my feet. "I'm not leaving you alone—not after what you did earlier."

I could see Dawn and Lora looking at each other and wondering what he meant by that.

Lurch continued, "I go to the bar—you go to the bar, Buddy boy!"

I wasn't going to argue with him, so I headed off to the bedroom to put my boots on. Somehow finding those boots wasn't as easy as I figured it would be. Meanwhile, Lurch was pressing the panic button—with good reason, I guess.

"Hey, man, you all right in there?"

"Yeah, be right out," I replied.

A couple of moments later, I went on out into the living room; and as I did; I noticed all of the others grinning from ear to ear.

Uh-huh, I thought warily. I get the picture. While I was in there getting my boots on, my old friend was in there telling tales out of school about my slurping down the iced tea. Okay, I thought, that's cool. This way if I should do something really off the wall, they'll all know why.

So off we went to Gulfport, out into the cool night air. By this time, to my immense relief, I was starting to feel like my old self again... I thought. I could just feel myself gaining tremendous energy. I was sure that the effects of the iced tea had worn off. Boy, the energy that I had that night. We hit the Rocks and two other bars, then for some reason, Dawn and Lora decided they had had enough, so we went on home. I had been sucking down quite a few beers, but thank goodness I was not driving.

When we got home, I stumbled into the kitchen and sat down to take off my boots. It was there, and then I noticed I only had on one boot!

"Hey, Lurch!" I yelled. "Hey, where did my other boot go? Did I leave it in your car?"

Now he was laughing uproariously. "No, it's not in my car. It was never in my car pal."

He walked from my bedroom into the kitchen and held up my boot. "Here it is, butthead, you never put it on." "You've been walking around all night with one boot on!"

"That's impossible," I said.

"No," he replied. What was nearly impossible was me telling everyone that saw you not to say anything!"

Why did I have to drink that tea? I thought. How could I have been so dumb not to ask Lurch what was in the tea? I should have known better, seeing how there was never anything in our fridge except beer to drink—ever!

I looked up at Lurch and said, "I'm going to bed, friend!" I said sarcastically. I threw myself on the bed fully clothed, and I was out like a light. After all, it has been almost twenty-four hours since I had slept. The night had surely been exhausting.

CHAPTER 4

Saturday morning had long since arrived, and most people were already up by then. I suppose it must've been around noon or one o'clock in the afternoon when my eyes finally popped open, and the first thing I hear is Lurch laughing! Even before I heard any of the words he was saying, I somehow knew that he was talking to someone about my adventures the night before. I strained my ears to hear and caught the words, "Didn't even know that he was only wearing one boot," followed by a rush of female laughter. Well, that was it. I had to get up now. Slowly, sleepily I groped my way past my drum set and on out into the living room. What a sight I must have been with me sleeping in jeans, bare chest, eyes at half mast, and messed-up hair hanging down my back and out to the side. I took one step into the living room and uttered those famous words: "Hey, I'm not proud!" Then, of course, the gales of laughter just began all the harder.

Lurch's female companions, as it turned out, were a girl whose name I would later learn was Caron and our old friend Kiki. Kiki was another of those kindred spirits that stopped in to visit from time to time. Lurch had met Kiki at a local hotspot called Dobb's House Diner one night and had invited her over to meet the crowd. That had been sometime before, and by now, she was a regular at our place; and every now and again, like our other regulars, she brought somebody else by. That was fine with us. It's sort of funny how back then we seemed to care for people before we even knew them. You were just automatically welcomed—until you did something to prove to us that you just weren't cool.

So Lurch and I were sort of automatically comfortable with Caron. The only problem seemed to be that she wasn't comfortable with us. She kept telling Kiki she wanted to leave, and of course, the rest of us were having a good time talking.

Finally, Kiki looked up at Caron and said, "Look, chick, I'm not ready to go, okay? When I'm ready to go, we'll go. Lurch and Buddy and I are talking," which Caron replied, sort of red in the face, "Fine! Just fine!

Just to relieve the tension a little, I turned to Lurch and said, "Hey, man, where is George at this morning?"

"He said he was going over to his mom's house this morning. He ought to be getting back pretty soon now. I gave him some money to pick up some beer for tonight."

"So what's happening tonight?" I asked.

Lurch looked at me as though I'd asked what direction the sun had come up. "What, are you new in town or something?" he asked. "What usually happens on Saturday night?"

"Well," I said innocently. "I guess probably a bunch of people will show up, and we'll party."

"Ah," he replied. "Welcome back!"

"Just don't give me any more of that tea," I told him.

"Hey, man," he replied. I didn't give you that tea. You did that all by yourself."

Just about that time, George pulled up in his preppy station wagon, and Lora and Dawn were with him as usual.

"Hey, all right!" I barked. "Some people."

"And what do you think we are?" demanded Kiki.

I didn't have a chance to reply because Lurch was saying, "That's all right, man, just remember one of those people is your new roommate."

"What are you talking about?" I asked. George has been our roommate for a long time now.

"Listen to Mr. Innocent," hooted Lurch. "For your information, butthead, I'm not talking about George. Don't you remember…you asked Dawn to move in with you?"

Then it came back to me. "Oh, yeah," I said after a short pause, then a long pause. "Hmmm, I guess I do remember that…vaguely… I think?"

You see the only problem, well, the main problem with Dawn was that she was loyal to no man. Way down deep she hated men—something which her sister told me once resulted from a very abusive father. She had seen her father beat her mother more than once, she had said. I don't know if that was true—I wasn't there—but I had no reason not to believe it. And come to think of it, I don't recall ever hearing anything about her mom or dad in all of the conversations that we'd had. Dawn and I did talk quite a bit, and that subject never came up. That was okay with me, of course; but if it was true, it may have explained why she was the way she was.

So anyway, in walked George and Lora, and Dawn.

"Hey, Smolsey," I jived to George. That was the nickname I had hung on him one night—don't ask me why. It just seemed to fit, and he seemed to like it, so what the hey!

Next I looked over at Lora. "Hey, girl…how are you?" Then, of course, I had to say something to Dawn as well. "*So*, how are you feeling this morning?" I could feel my face turning three shades of red at the same time. One thing was for sure: I didn't know how she was going to respond to me that morning. Hey, maybe she had just forgotten the whole thing. I glanced over at Lurch and saw that he was practically biting a hole in his lip trying not to laugh. He knew that I really didn't want Dawn to move in, and he also knew that I had really gotten myself in deep this time; and of course, he was enjoying every minute of it. Of course, if our roles had been reversed, I would have been acting exactly the same way—or maybe even a little worse. I think if the tables had been turned, I would probably have come up with something really good like, "Hey, Dawn… I thought maybe you'd have brought some clothes with you?"

On the other hand, her living here might not be all that bad. I mean I could just take it for what it was worth and sort of follow my instincts. Hell, I'd never lived with a girl before! This was unexplored territory. I might as well check it out to see what it would be like. One thing was for sure: I was not going to tell her that I hadn't really meant to ask her. I just flat out did not want to hurt her feelings. I did not like being mean to people—guess I got that from my mom.

Meanwhile, Dawn was standing there in front of me, sort of biting her lip; and if I'd been a little less upset about the dubious prospect of being her roommate, I could have seen that something was seriously wrong—as far as she was concerned.

"Buddy," she said. "I... I really need to talk to you."

Oh my goodness, I thought. *Reprieve! She's changed her mind about moving in, and she wants to break it to me gently!*

I stepped in and put my arm around her. "Sure, baby," I said. Let's go into the bedroom and talk?" Then I looked around at the others in the room. "You folks will excuse us, won't you?"

It was then that I noticed a tear rolling slowly down her lightly freckled cheek. "Buddy, I'm serious," she said softly but sternly. "I need to talk to you...seriously!"

That certainly got my attention. "Okay," I said softly and slowly, trying to get a handle on the situation. "Let's go out to the kitchen and talk."

So out to the kitchen we went. I sat down at the table, and she, still standing, turned and stared out the window.

"What's got you so upset?" I asked. I was prepared for anything except for what happened next. She burst into tears. I didn't know what to say, so I came up with something that she probably did not want to hear.

I said, "Look. If you don't wanna move in then... I understand. I mean...you know it was a spur of the moment."

"My kids!" she sobbed. "My kids are gone!"

Hearing this, I stood up and gently put my arm around her. Surprises were really starting to pile up now. "What? What do you mean gone?"

Saying the words seemed to have strengthened her a little. She pushed out of my arms and walked over and tore off a paper towel. She blew her nose and wiped her eyes. She was still sniffling a little as she continued. "My husband...my ex, I mean. He came over last night when we were at the Rocks and took the children. He took them to his house. Then he told my grandmother that I should not try to get them back." Then she looked back out the kitchen window. Somehow that seemed to have a calming effect on her.

Meanwhile, I was in desperate need of something to calm me down. "Just a moment," I said. "Excuse me just a second…" I went back into the living room, running my fingers desperately through my hair. All of the others stared at me. They were wondering, I guess, just what it was that Dawn had shared with me—except for George and Lora; I figured they already knew by this time.

"Kiki," I blared. "Can I have one of your beers?"

"Why sure," she said, taking a can out of the sack that was in front of her. "They're not very cold, but you're welcome to it."

Looking concerned as she handed me the beer, she said, "Hey, Buddy…is everything all right in there?"

Why is it the only time people ask if it's all right is when they know perfectly well that it's not? I just threw up my hands.

"Well, no, not really. It's a long story. I'll tell you later, okay?" And with that, I headed back to the kitchen.

As soon as I got back there, Dawn reached for my beer, took a healthy slug of it, then handed it back to me. "Oh, Buddy," she wailed, snuggling up against me. "What am I gonna do? What am I gonna do?"

And now I was thinking, *What am I gonna do?* All I could do was just shake my head and say, "I don't know, baby, I just don't know." And I really didn't know. Hey, I had just turned twenty. I'd never been in a situation like this before. Way back deep somewhere in my brain, I was asking myself why the sudden concern for her children when up until now, when her ex had shown up and spirited them away, I had never seen them all together. Did she really care that much about them, I wondered? Was she just pissed that another man had done something to hurt her again? Now, thinking long and hard, it wasn't really easy to do because of the way she was standing up so close against me.

"Hey," I said. "I know what you can do. Just get out your divorce papers! Surely it says something about who gets the kids, you know, who is in charge of them and all."

26

She looked up at me and then down at the floor. "No," she muttered faintly. "No, that won't do any good…"

That sort of puzzled me, but I went on. "Well…do you remember anything that the judge said?"

"What judge?" she said awkwardly, looking down at the floor.

"What judge?" I echoed stupidly. I looked down into her face— or at least trying to—and I said slowly, measurably, "Look, I've never been divorced. I have no idea what it's like or what goes on, okay? I just figured there had to be a judge in there somewhere…look, I'm just trying to help!"

"Oh, Buddy, I know you are," she murmured softly. "And believe me, I am grateful. It's just that…well…" Finally, she tipped her face up toward me and looked me straight in the eye, and with a deep breath, she said, "There was no divorce. We're just separated."

I couldn't believe it! I just plain could not believe it. And yet here she was, looking me in the eyes, and she had never looked in my eyes before. That must mean that she was telling the truth. Besides, why would she lie about something like that? I'm sure that shock and disbelief must have been written all over my face. Looking back on it, it must have been very hard for her to have said those words to me. It seems like we stood there and stared at each other for about five minutes, me still confused and her waiting for my response.

Finally, I managed to blurt out, "You're not divorced? You're married? You're still married?"

Meanwhile, she had shifted her eyes back down to the floor. "Well…not exactly. I'm almost divorced," she said.

"Not exactly!" I roared. I'm sure they must have heard me in the living room. "Almost divorced? It's like being a little bit pregnant… either you are or you aren't!"

"Well, Buddy…you know what I mean! It's not like we were ever going to get back together again or anything…"

"How do I know that?" I responded. "How do I know anything about you now, for that matter! Why did you lie about it?"

She gave a big sigh. "I don't know," she said. "I guess I sort of thought…well, I guess I figured that if you knew I was married, you wouldn't have asked me out."

I fired back. "I've never asked you out! You and I have just kind of ended up together somehow at parties or bars or whatever..."

"Are you mad at me?" she asked shyly. "I guess you have a right to be, but..." she left the sentence unfinished.

I just stood there for a moment, looking down at her and thinking. Finally, I said, "I guess I don't really know how I feel. Maybe my brain is still a little numb from last night." I took another minute to sort of think things out. "But... I suppose if I was mad I'd know it, so I must not be that mad."

Her arms came around me now, and she snuggled even closer. "I'm glad to hear that," she said dreamily.

I looked down, and now her eyes were closed.

She asked, "Do you know what I really want to do?"

I sort of gritted my teeth because I knew what was coming.

"I just want to stay here with you and get my shit together."

A little grimace passed over my face as her theme phrase stumbled out over her lips. I got so tired of that phrase—but I held back the acerbic comment I was about to make and simply said, "Yeah, okay."

Then we kissed. Actually, we kissed for a good long while, and all the time we were kissing, I was thinking this is nice; but nice as it was, I also knew that she had deliberately lied to me about her marriage. I had no idea then that this was just the beginning of her deception so far as I was concerned.

Our deep kiss was interrupted then by Lurch's foghorn voice. "Hey, you two, get your pants on. I'm coming in!"

True to his promise, he came through the door, and the smile on his face was as wide as a barn door. "Hey, you guys, what are you doing out here anyway, planning your wedding?"

Dawn and I glanced quickly at each other, then by mutual consent, away. Of all the times to bring that subject up! I shook my head quickly at Lurch. "Wrong question, man!" I said. He knew by the tone of my voice that I meant it.

He walked on over to the refrigerator, and upon opening it, he said, "Hey, what happened to the beer you guys were supposed to get?"

"Oh!" Dawn replied. "I guess it's still in George's car."

Sarcastically Lurch snapped back, "Well, it's not doing any good out there!"

Then Dawn, looking at Lurch, said, "I feel like partying tonight." Then looking at me, she said with a smile, "And I don't have to leave tonight either."

"Oh," grumbled Lurch in a questioning tone of voice as he looked over at me, a little dumb grin on his face.

"Oh? Oh! No!" said Dawn in a sort of defiant declaratory tone. "I am staying with my Buddy tonight!"

"Well," said Lurch mockingly with that broad, broad smile spreading across his face once again. "Ain't that sweet?"

I, for my part, looked a warning toward him. "Hey, man," I said with a little edge in my voice. "Save it, okay, just save it!"

We all went back into the living room then, and Dawn told Lora that she thought the two of them should go get some kind of food for lunch. Lora was glad to hear it because George was taking a shower, which left her all alone in that room with Lurch, Kiki, and Kiki's charming friend Caron. Lora was basically a shy person, but the truth of the matter was that even if she had been an extrovert of the extroverts, she would have had absolutely nothing in common with that crowd. Everybody pitched in a few bucks, then we told them to get some cigarettes and some Boone's Farm (which was popular in the day).

As Lora scribbled it down, she looked up with a weary little frown on her face. "Do you people ever eat?"

We all laughed partly because of what she had said and partly because it was the first thing that she'd really said all day.

Then Lurch blurted out, "Hey, yeah, get some chips too!"

Lora just looked down at her list again and shook her head slowly back and forth. I'm not sure that potato chips were what she had in mind.

"Okay," said Dawn, grabbing the stash and her purse and heading toward the door. "We'll be back!"

Lurch's reply was typical: "Thanks for the warning!"

By this time, George was getting out of the shower, and—wonder of wonders!—Kiki's friend Caron was starting to mellow a bit.

Apparently, she had given up on leaving. Kiki would go in her own time and not before. So she started thumbing through our records, looking for some music to put on.

"Boy, you guys sure have a lot of records," she said in a wondering tone of voice.

"Yeah, they're Lurch's," I replied. "He stole them all," which wasn't really true, but I really needed to get a rise out of him.

Meanwhile, Kiki turned toward me in a confidential sort of way—and I knew exactly what she was going to say. She didn't disappoint me in the slightest. So she said, a little smile playing around the corners of her mouth, "So what's with you and this Dawn chick?"

I made a little palms-up gesture. "Who knows?" I said. "Least of all me. This has been the craziest weekend. Let me fill you in on a little of what's been happening to me in the last twenty-four hours. Okay, I came home Friday afternoon and accidentally drank some of Lurch's electric iced tea. So then I go off on my first and last LSD trip, and somewhere in the middle of it, I figured that it was a good idea to ask her to move in with me.

"Then I go out barhopping with this idiot"—pointing to Lurch, who immediately started snickering—"and I was so messed up from the tea that I did not realize that I was only wearing one boot. And naturally, my boy here didn't bother telling me about it because he was having so much fun watching me make an ass of myself.

"So finally I get to bed about four this morning, and I actually woke up in a pretty good mood, and then this guy here tells me about my asking Dawn to move in with me, which I somehow missed in all of the excitement. Then to top it all off…about an hour into my day, I find out that I've been sleeping with a married woman!" I gave a shrug. "Just a typical boring weekend here at the asylum."

At this, Lurch whipped around, his crooked jaw practically dragging on the ground. "Oh wow!" he said sarcastically. "She's married? Is nothing sacred?"

"Well," I said more than a little indignantly. "That may be funny to you, but all this time I thought she was divorced!"

George was making his way into the room by this time, his freshly washed hair sticking out a little.

"I knew she was still married," he said quietly.

I stared at him. "Well, hey... Smolsey!" I said a little bitterly. "Thanks a lot, friend!"

He looked at me curiously and said, "I don't see why the hell it matters anyway. I mean, after all, you're not proud, are you?" And then he smiled a little smile and continued. "Or are you?"

"That's not it at all, man," I said. "I mean I have this thing about messing around with another man's woman. I don't want it done to me, so I don't do it to anybody else."

Lurch gave a cackle. "Well, it looks like you're doing it now, aren't you?" Then he must have seen the look on my face because he continued, "But hey, man, I guess you really didn't know. I mean, how could you have known?"

I looked over reproachfully at George. Still feeling betrayed, I said, "Yeah, how would I have known?"

"Well," interjected Kiki. "If you ask me, and I know that you didn't, but if you ask me, I don't think that you should let it bother you. I mean it doesn't seem to be bothering her any, and she sure as hell knew."

"Yeah... I guess so," I said, lighting the day's first cigarette. "I guess so."

What Kiki had said about Dawn certainly seemed to be true. The fact that she was married didn't seem to bother her at all; and if she could do this to her husband, what sort of head games would she be playing on me? Hell, maybe she was playing them with me right now. And what about those kids—the ones she'd been so concerned about earlier? She certainly seemed to have gotten over that crisis in a hurry.

Now the girls had gotten back with some food and Lurch's chips. They had bought bread, lunch meat, cheese, and mayonnaise to make sandwiches. Dawn made a sandwich for me and for her, and we sat down at the kitchen table and ate. After that, I looked at her and informed her that I was really tired and I was going to lie down for a while. She said she would join me, and the two of us lay down on the bed, and it wasn't long before we were sound asleep in each other's arms.

CHAPTER 5

I finally woke up at about four to the sound of music playing in the living room. Dawn had woken up before me and went on out to join the crowd. I found my cleanest shirt to put on and stumbled on out to meet our guests. Out in the living room were Lurch, Dawn, Lora, and George. Kiki and Caron had long been gone.

Dawn looked up and said, "Hey, look who's awake."

I was actually expecting a little better greeting than that from my new steady. Oh well! I went into the kitchen, opened the fridge, and grabbed a beer then returned to the living room and sat down on the couch next to her.

About that time, there was a knock on the door, which was strange because nobody ever knocked on our door.

Lurch looked at me and said, "Are you going to answer that?"

"What, you're suddenly a cripple?"

Lora then jumped up and said, "I'll get the door. Just stay where you're at."

She opened the door, and in staggered our friend Phil. He took one look at Lora and said, "Hey, baby, where'd you come from?"

Lurch then jumped up because he could tell she was really scared of this guy. Lurch went over and stood between him and Lora and, pointing with his hand, said, "Come on in, man." Then before Lurch could head him off, he went over and sat in Lurch's favorite green chair.

Phil was sort of a throwback. To begin with, he was a skinny little skeleton of a guy—skinnier than Lurch, really—but Lurch seemed skinnier because he was so tall. Phil had been in prison, busted for selling drugs as Lurch had also been.

The music that we were playing indicated it would probably be a beer-drinking night—good old rock 'n' roll with the likes of ZZ Top, James Gang, Heart, J Geils. All indications were that a typical Saturday night was about to erupt. People were beginning to drift in at about the usual rate—one or two each half hour. Someone would come and someone would go. Things would usually be at peak capacity around eleven, then around midnight, more and more folks would begin to leave until things finally broke up around 1:00 or 2:00 a.m. This night was no different.

Around midnight, some of us decided we would drive down to the 7-Eleven to get some munchies. One of the funniest sites in the world is a carload of stoned people with the munchies walking around a 7-Eleven with inane giggles and red eyes picking out their Oreos and chocolate milk, RC cola and moon pies, or taco-flavored Doritos. Then there was always somebody that wanted to borrow $0.50 so he could buy a Three Musketeers bar for later. I could never understand that one. If I bought something, I ate it right then and there. There was no later!

Back to the house we headed. We walked into the living room to the sound of Phil snoring loudly. We tried to wake him up, but we really didn't have any luck. He was out for the count. He was also sprawled out in our favorite chair. We weren't really happy about that.

Then George chimed in. "Hey, I've got an idea! Let's not wake him up. Let's carry him—chair and all—out into the front yard."

Now a sneaky smile was starting to emerge from everyone's face.

"Okay, let's do it," I ordered.

It was a good thing Phil was so skinny because the chair was really heavy. It took three of us to get him up and out the door.

We finally got him out into the front yard and picked a spot close to the sidewalk that we figured was just hilarious. We were so proud of ourselves.

We had turned and started to walk in the house when Lurch stopped and said, "Guys, let's move him out a little bit further so he'll be sitting at the bus stop!"

Yes, there was also a bus stop on the corner where we lived.

"Yeah," George cheered, pumping his fist in the air.

Of course, we all agreed, and up Phil and the chair went to the bus stop. He had not stirred a bit, so we all went back into the house, laughing as we went.

George asked, "What time does the bus come by?"

"I don't think it runs past midnight," I said.

So we all agreed it was time to just turn in, and we also agreed it was one hell of a prank.

As we walked into the house, Dawn was standing, looking out the window at Phil. "Hey, do you know what else we could do? We could call the cops and tell them there's someone sitting in our yard in a big chair."

All three of us—George, Lurch, and I—snapped our heads around in disbelief to stare at her.

"What's a matter with you, girl?" George snapped at her. "Are you on drugs?" which, of course, she might have been.

"That's all we need, baby," I said, shaking my head in wonderment. "To bring the heat down on us! That would be great, wouldn't it? Maybe we could invite them in and have a beer with them!"

"I'm sorry," Dawn whimpered. "I guess I wasn't thinking straight."

Then Lurch, trying to make light of the situation, turned and said, "Besides…we don't even have a telephone."

"I don't know about you, guys," I said. "But I am ready for bed." I walked down the hallway toward my bedroom. Then I looked back and said half-jokingly, "And don't try anything tonight, Dawn. I'm not in the mood!"

I decided to at least take off the clothes I had slept in the night before and put on a pair of shorts and a T-shirt. Lord knew I could use some decent sleep right about now with the weekend I was having, which, come to think of it, wasn't all that much different from any other weekend. I pulled back the sheets, wondering whether or not she would join me. She had said that she was going to, but then of course, Dawn said a lot of things.

Well, we will just have to wait and see, I thought. *We'll just have to…wait…and…*

She never made it.

CHAPTER 6

You need to understand what Sunday morning was like for us. To begin with, of course, it was always the day after the night before; and in addition, well, it was Sunday morning. Sunday mornings were always just a super-relaxed time around the homestead. We weren't exactly known for our early hours, but Sunday morning was a time when we always slept late—all three of us—I mean eleven o'clock, twelve o'clock sleeping late. Then we'd get up and sort of drift out to the living room at our own paces, pour a cup of coffee and light a cigarette, and just sit around and talk about who did what to who? Which of us got the highest? And there was always at least one story about "I can't believe what you did last night!" Sitting around and talking with my roomies on Sunday mornings under those laid-back circumstances was always very relaxing to me, and I genuinely looked forward to it. We really got to know each other in those sessions.

This particular Sunday morning, however, it would not start out being relaxed at all. All of a sudden, there was this terrible noise, and the only thing I could think of for a moment was that maybe we were being raided by the police or something. It wasn't the police— just a six-foot-four, 120-pound jackass named Lurch. *Bang bang bang bang!* The noise was deafening. I sat up in my bed as if I'd been ejected from a jet plane.

I clamped my hands over my ears and just screamed, "*Stop it!* Stop, you son of a bitch!"

Meanwhile, here was Lurch, parading around my bedroom with a hammer in one hand and a kitchen pot in the other and hitting one against the other as he sang in an inane voice: "It's time to get up! It's time to get up! It's time to get up in the morning!"

And then he stopped and looked over at me with a mock-concerned look on his face. "Oh, Buddy boy," sympathy dripping from his voice. "Did I wake you up? I'm sorry."

"I'll make you sorry, you…" I knew a lot of choice names back then, but I honestly couldn't think of one that was bad enough to call him. I pointed at the nightstand. "I don't know why you had to do that, but let me tell you one thing. If there was a gun in this drawer, you'd be a dead man right now! Why the hell—"

My words were interrupted when Dawn poked her head around the door frame, all smiles and sweetness and summertime flowers. "Breakfast is served in the dining room," she said, a grin on her face. "I guess you heard the dinner bell?"

"Oh, this is great," I growled. "You two are a regular Abbott and Costello. Tell me, girl…what happened to you last night? I thought you were coming to bed?"

She just stood there, batting her eyes with Shirley Temple's innocence. "Well," she simpered. "I was just going along with what you said when you went to bed—you know, about not trying anything."

Anything I would have said at that point would have been drowned out by the geyser of laughter coming from these two.

"I know what you meant, Buddy," she said. "But the truth of it is Lurch and I got to talking out in the living room, and we ended up staying up all night."

"Ah," I said. "That's why you two are acting so goofy. You're still messed up from last night." I reached up and grabbed my watch from the nightstand and looked at it. "Nine fifteen!" It was practically the middle of the night.

Then all of a sudden, I caught the scent of something cooking. "Bacon! Is that bacon I smell?"

Dawn, meanwhile, had lain down on the bed next to me. She smiled over at me. "Yes," she said and checked the items off on her fingers as she named them: "Bacon, eggs, and biscuits."

"The biscuits were my idea," said Lurch, grinning.

"Where's George," I asked. "Is he out there too?"

Lurch shook his head. "Naw... I really don't know where he is. He crashed right after you did last night, but he was gone by the time we got back from our little shopping trip... I was still a little groggy from sleep."

"So what did you two do after I went to bed?"

"Just sat and talked?" Dawn piped up. "That was basically it until we decided to go to Gulfport and stop at my grandma's house and had coffee with her. It was on the way back that I got the idea about making breakfast." Then she got up off the bed and gave a little nod with her head toward the other part of the house. "So, come on, let's eat!"

We were just finishing up our breakfast that Sunday morning when George returned. He came out into the kitchen, took a shocked look at the table, and said, "Damn, somebody cooked?"

I guess it was a little hard for him to comprehend, seeing how we never cooked breakfast before.

"Yeah, we decided to cook a real meal for once," I said.

Lurch just gave me a long hard stare. "Have you ever heard such lying in your life?" he turned to George. "Buddy didn't cook anything. It was me and Dawn that cooked the breakfast. But sorry, it's all gone."

George replied, "Oh, that's all right. I ate at my mom's house this morning." He grabbed the spare chair and sat down to join us. "By the way, I gave Phil a ride home this morning. He came stumbling in about seven o'clock, wondering how he got out on the lawn."

Dawn had, it seemed, chosen the wrong moment to take a sip of coffee. At the mention of Phil, she began giggling and chortling, and I was half afraid for a moment that I was going to get an unplanned shower. She managed to get things under control, however and afterward she asked, "So what did you tell him?"

George shrugged and said, "I told him that I had no idea, but what I was really wondering was how he managed to get that big heavy chair out there by himself." George was waiting for the laughter to die down before he hit us with the topper. "He told me he always was a wiry little guy!"

When the laughter died down from that, he and I decided that we'd better go out and retrieve the chair. After all, it was our best one.

When we went out, I noticed this huge collection of old folks out on the porch of the convalescent center across the street. In all the time I'd been living in that house, I had never seen more than three people at a time on that porch. Yet this morning, however, there were at least a dozen. Then as we went over to the chair, I heard gentle laughter from across the street, and looking over, I saw an old man standing there, pointing to us and laughing. Somehow, that rankled me. I've never liked being laughed at by anyone.

I nudged George. "You see that? Why are they laughing at us?"

He gave a quick shake of his head. "No, man, you got it wrong. They're not laughing at us. They're laughing at Phil. You know how early old people wake up. They probably saw him sitting out there... sitting at the bus stop, and they're just sort of enjoying it all over again. God, Buddy! I mean, old people don't have that much to laugh at you know?" Let 'm enjoy whatever they can."

I'm glad that he was there to make that comment because somehow, it put things into an entirely new perspective for me. He was right—life must get pretty boring over there. They probably watched us from across the street for any spice that we could put into their lives. After all, they hadn't been born old. I was sure that they could appreciate a good prank as much as the next guy.

"Hey, Buddy, where did you go all of a sudden?" It was George, nudging at my elbow, breaking in on my daydreams. "Come on, man, grab a hold of this chair. We haven't got all day!"

I grabbed a hold on the chair, of course, and we carried it on toward the house; but as we were about to go into the house, I couldn't help but look back across the street to our audience and grin and give them a victory wave. They waved back! It was cool! It was like having a bunch of kindred spirits right across the street.

When I went back into the house, I headed back toward the bathroom and saw Dawn back in my room, sort of checking it out.

"What are you doing back here?" I asked. Not that I really had to. After all, I pretty much knew.

"Oh," she said. "Just sort of…looking things over." She looked up at me. "There's not much space in here, is there?"

"Tell me about it," I said.

"I was thinking about going over to Granny's to get some of my clothes to bring over," she said. She was looking sort of sideways at me now, seeing what I'd say to that. She gave a glance around the room. "Maybe we could get another dresser?"

"We," I echoed. "We could get another dresser?" Why was I so surprised? It's just that it sounded so permanent somehow, so scary.

"Well, I'm gonna need something," she said. "And these drums! These drums have got to go! Maybe we could put them out on the street like we did Phil!" She was teasing me now, playing with me, but I didn't pick up on it at the time.

I stared over at her. "If anybody goes out on the street, it'll be you!"

At that, she just sort of turned and walked out of the room; and I, of course, felt guilty.

"Hey." I took a hold of her arm. "Don't go away mad!"

She jerked her arm away and said, "I know, I know. Just go away, right?"

Either there was a tear in her eye, or I was imagining it. Either way, I didn't much like it. Fortunately, my suave sophistication took over. "Hey, girl," I said. "Who loves you, baby?" It was a tear.

"Look, I've got to go over to Granny's," she said, stumbling down the hall. "See ya later."

I walked on out into the living room and looked out the window as she drove away. Lurch was coming out of the kitchen.

"Where is she going?"

"Over to Granny's," I replied in a distracted tone of voice, still looking after her.

"Well, is she coming back?"

I just shook my head. "I haven't the slightest idea," I said slowly.

Suddenly I was very, very tired. I turned to face him. "Look, I'm going back to bed, okay? And…do me a favor? Don't wake me up for lunch!"

CHAPTER 7

Now, mind you, every weekend that we spent at that house wasn't as crazy as some of the others were. Some were just ordinary, laid-back weekends. On the other hand, some were just downright mystifying, and I suppose I'll never remember the really wild ones—which brings to mind one episode that might well have been my last.

I was working as an electrician apprentice for a company. We were working on a pretty big project at the time. We were refurbishing an old abandoned grocery store into (get this) a mail-order drug warehouse. The idea was to receive prescriptions from people by mail and, in turn, mail the drug orders out. That would make it nice for the older folks who had trouble getting out. Of course, it also made it nice for a couple of freaks posing as electricians.

I was working that day—it was a Thursday, as I remember—with a guy they called "Jake the Polock. I had just met Jake a couple of days before. A few of the drug warehouse employees were in that day, stocking the shelves and getting ready to open for business. Jake and I were up on a scissor lift, hooking up all the long rows of fluorescent lights in the building. As we wired up the lights and put the bulbs in, we sort of, well, browsed through all those bottles of pills that we kinda had access to. I didn't know what Jake was looking for, but I thought it would be nice if I could find something that was good for partying. The thing about it was we weren't all that sure as to what all the stuff was. I found myself wishing that Lurch was there; he would have known just where to go.

So what it came down to is as we were installing the lights, we were more or less casing the joint. Finally, I spotted a bottle with the word *phenobarbital* on it. Somehow that sort of rang a bell with me.

"Hey, Jake," I whispered. We had to be really careful with those employees of the store there after all. "I think I found something good over here."

"What is it?" he whispered back.

"It's called phenobarbital," I replied. I reached in on the shelf just far enough to turn the bottle around so that he could see the label.

"Hmm...no, I don't think that's worth taking. It's only sixty-five milligrams." Jake gave me a little shrug.

"Yeah," I answered back. "But if you do two or three of them, I bet you could get off. So what are we going to put them in?" I questioned.

You have to understand these were big wholesale-size containers we were dealing with. Each bottle contained around one thousand pills. Jake looked around for a couple of seconds, then his eyes lit on a box of self-tapping screws. "Just the thing," he said.

He dumped the screws into his nail apron and then looked at me. "Put some in here...careful though," and he looked around slowly to see if anyone was watching.

I reached in, grabbed the bottle, and pulled off the lid. "Damn it!" There was a big wad of cotton underneath the cap. I should have known. Jake gave me a little chuckle as I was setting myself up to the task of getting that cotton out of the container.

Jake whispered urgently, "Hey, someone's coming. Man, things are really getting tense!"

Hastily I set the lid on the bottle and put the bottle back on the shelf just before this middle-aged woman came cruising around the corner. I'm pretty sure that she was suspicious of us. Gee, I wonder why. Two long-haired hippie types with facial hair—I know it's not right to stereotype people, but come on!

"Working hard today, fellows?" she asked. And was is it my imagination, or was there an odd little smile on her face?

Jake and I both answered awkwardly and at the same time. "Yes…yes, ma'am!"

"Well"—she smiled that funny smile again—"well, don't work too hard." Then she just walked on by.

Jake and I both took a deep breath, exhaled, and with our exhalation let out a heartfelt "Wow!" You would've thought we had rehearsed it.

"Thanks for the warning," I whispered to Jake. "How does it look now?"

"Coast is clear," he said. Not that I didn't trust him, but I looked around for myself just to be sure. Then I pulled out my needle-nose pliers.

Enough of this fooling around, I thought. I grabbed a hold of that cotton wad and yanked it out properly this time, still sort of looking around for any "big brothers" who might be around. I opened up the screw box and filled it about halfway with the pills. Then I put the cotton back into the bottle, popped on the lid, and put the bottle back on the shelf. I handed the screw box to Jake, and he stashed it in the bottom of his tool bucket.

"We did it," I whispered.

Jake was sweating like a stuck pig, but he managed a little smile.

"Tell you what, man, after work today, we'll go over to my house and have a couple of beers. If my roommate is home, he can probably tell us all about these pills."

"All right," Jake enthused. "Sounds good to me."

It was finally coming up on quitting time, and while we were cleaning up and getting ready to go home, we made our plans. Lurch was working a lot farther from home than I was, so he was using my car—an old Oldsmobile Holiday that my brother-in-law had given me. Jake was driving a company van, so we drove that back to the shop and took Jake's car to the house. As we pulled up, I saw the Holiday parked by the curb where we usually parked.

"Oh good," I said. "Lurch is already home."

"Lurch?" Jake said, giving me an inquiring look as he shut off the engine.

"Yeah," I said. "It's not his real name, but that's what everybody calls him. You'll understand once you see him."

"What's his real name?" Jake asked. "I'd tell you his real name, but you wouldn't believe it. Just stay with Lurch," I said. "Trust me."

We walked on into the house, and I made the necessary introductions. "Hey, Lurch," I said. "We got something here that we want you to look at, man." I pulled out the box of pills, setting them on the table.

"At your service!" said Lurch. He really took pride in his knowledge of pills. What a pharmaceutical worker he would have been! "What you got here?" he said, opening the box and reaching inside.

"Phenobarbitals," I replied. "But they're only sixty-five milligrams, though."

"Hmm," Lurch said thoughtfully, rolling a few of the pills around in his hands like worry beads. "I've heard of these before, but with that low milligram count…hey, man, I don't know. He thought about it for a moment then looked decisively up at me. Well, there's only one real way to find out, I guess. Let me have a couple of them, and I'll run them (shoot up) tonight and let you know tomorrow."

"Sounds good to me," I said. Then I looked across to Jake. "What do you say?"

Jake shrugged. "Sure," he said. "Why not?"

So we busied ourselves with splitting up the pills that remained.

Jake had just walked out the door with his little stash of pills when Dawn came down the hall. She was sharing my bedroom by this time. She walked out wearing this orange-and-brown dress. She gave me a little preening twirl as if she were a fashion model or something and grinned over at me. "How do you like it?" she said proudly, obviously inviting a compliment.

"It's great," I said. "Wonderful! Suits you to a T!" Then I paused for a moment and asked, "Tell me…what exactly are we talking about?"

"Oh," she said, giving me a little poke in the stomach. "It's my uniform. I got a job!" Obviously, she was very excited about it. "Oh," I said whimsically. "Where are you working, Tacky Dresses 'R' Us?"

She gave me a stare.

"My, are you in a mood today!"

"No, for your information. I got a job as a waitress at Frisches in Pasadena, and I am very excited about it!" She gave a sigh. "Who knows? "Maybe it will help me get my shit together."

"Hey, I'm working there too," piped up Lurch. "I'm going to be the dishwasher. It'll be great," he said. "I hate getting up and going to work in the morning. I've always been a night person. Besides, I can ride to work with Dawn, and you can have your car back."

So that's why he had been home early? Meanwhile, I was just sort of sitting there, pondering all these changes. I looked over to Dawn. "So…when do you start work?"

"We start tonight," she said. "We were supposed to start tomorrow, but they are really shorthanded, so we agreed to come in tonight. We'll be working from four till midnight." She looked down at her watch. "We are going to be late today because I had to go and pick up my uniforms."

"Wait a minute," I questioned. "You don't get off until midnight?"

"That's what I just said," she barked, adopting a little defensive tone in her voice. "So what's wrong with that?"

"Oh, nothing, nothing. It's just that we won't see each other much."

"I'll see you when I get home," she said, trying to convince me.

"Yeah, and when will that be?" I asked.

Now, sort of tilting her eyes up toward the ceiling, she said, "Well, probably closer to one because we have to stay and clean up."

"Oh nice," I said sarcastically. "You'll be home by one, that is if you decide to come home. And even then, I'll be asleep in bed because I have to get up at five thirty. Yeah, that should work out just fine."

"Look," said Lurch, jumping in. "I hate to interrupt this lovers' spat, but we really need to get going. You can discuss it later—that is if you ever see each other again," he said, laughing as he headed toward the door.

The next thing I knew, they were gone, and George was off somewhere who knew where. He probably wouldn't be in all evening, and there I was stuck by myself. I felt abandoned! I mean there was always somebody home—but here I was all alone. I decided not to worry about it. I had a couple more beers then went in and beat on my drums for a while. It wasn't long until I got tired of that, so I showered then listened to some records—but it was still only eight o'clock. Okay, I'll just go lie down and try to catch a few zees then get up later when the gang comes home from work. So off I went to bed, but I might as well have been sitting in the living room for all the sleep I got. You know how it goes—a tiny little thought comes into your mind, and it just sort of eats away at you; and before you know it, you're wider and wider awake.

And you know what I was thinking about that night—or rather who? I had never been able to figure that girl out, but it was becoming more and more impossible all the time. She was really starting to play with my head these days. It seemed like we were only getting along when she wanted to get along—and that was getting to be less and less frequent. It wasn't that I really suspected Lurch of anything behind my back, but the fact remains that he was spending a lot more time with her than I was. Maybe I was just starting to get too involved with her? When this whole thing started with her moving in with me, I had decided to just take it for what it was worth. Well, it sure as hell didn't seem to be worth an awful lot anymore. Sure, we were sharing a bedroom—big deal. Now she would be sleeping in the bed during the day, and I would be sleeping there at night. At least maybe she'll wake me up when she gets home, I remember thinking. I actually found myself looking forward to that. Maybe I did care for her more than I let myself believe that I did.

I finally did manage to drop off to sleep, and the next thing I knew, it was morning. I stirred lazily and reached over for Dawn beside me—but she wasn't there—and then it began again, that awful feeling I had gone to bed with the night before. But this time, the heartache was accompanied by anger that slowly built within me.

I got up, and as I was getting dressed, I was muttering under my breath. "I am getting so sick of this crap! This is it! This is all! I am not going to put up with this any longer!"

I was furious by this time and getting madder by the second! I stalked out of my bedroom toward the bathroom, and out of the corner of my eye, I saw her. She was curled up on the couch with a blanket, sleeping, looking so sweet and innocent. It seemed kind of strange not to see her holding onto a Raggedy Ann or something tucked in beside her.

I walked over to the couch and looked down at her. A cylindrical mound of ashes in the ashtray showed where she lit a cigarette and put it down then had fallen asleep or maybe passed out before she could smoke it, a half-full Tom Collins glass (one that I had never seen before) sitting next to the ashtray on the coffee table, a slice of lemon still floating in the glass. It didn't take much to put two and two together. Ready to explode, I reached down and shook her by the shoulder.

"Well, did you have a good time at work last night? I didn't realize that place served mixed drinks!"

She was now stretching out and slowly waking up. She opened her eyes, blinking groggily, then grinned up at me. "Oh, hi, Buddy." The way she was talking, I could tell that she was still about half loaded.

"Funny thing," I said. "When you left for work yesterday, I could have sworn that you said that you'd see me when you got home?" I paused and looked down at my watch. "Don't tell me you're just now getting home?"

"What? No." The look on her face went from a blank one to a confused one. "What...what time is it?" She blinked, still trying to come fully awake. "Are you mad at me, Buddy?" Her tone implied that such a feeling on my part was beyond her understanding.

"Just answer me one thing, Dawn," I said slowly. "Are you and I supposed to be together or not? Don't ask me why, but I was kind of wanting to see you when you got in last night. I was sort of expecting to wake up with a warm body next to me—but that didn't happen, did it? Instead, you decided you'd rather sleep on this old worn-out couch than with me!"

She raised herself up. "Oh, Buddy, you are mad at me."

"Gee, why would you say that?" I asked.

47

Then she stood up and sort of leaned into me, putting her arms around me. "Oh, Buddy, I'm sorry. I stayed out here because I didn't want to disturb you. After all, I knew you had to get up early to go to work… I certainly didn't mean to upset you. I really am sorry."

But I noticed that she wasn't looking me in the eye. I pulled away from her slowly. "Look," I said, a little calmer by this time. "I really don't know what's going on here, but I do know this—you and I need to sit down together and figure out just what is going on with us. We hardly see each other anymore, and the worst part of it is that you just don't seem to mind!"

She gave a little shake of her head. "Come on now, Buddy, that's just not true. I do still care about you—you know that I do."

"I really don't have time to talk about this right now, Dawn. I have to get ready. So where's Lurch?" I asked.

Dawn had meanwhile lain back down on the couch; I guess she liked it better than a bed. Pointing to the kitchen, she said, "He's in there with Son."

"Oh, okay," I said, heading for the bathroom but then I stopped. *Son?* I thought. I turned back around and looked at her. "Who is Son?"

"Oh," she answered. "We met him at work. He's one of the busboys."

Now we were all the time meeting people in different places and bringing them home with us. There was nothing new about that, but I decided that I wasn't in that big of a hurry to get to work, so I headed toward the kitchen to check this dude out. I sauntered on into the kitchen, and there was Lurch, talking with this kid who looked to be several years the other side of shaving. It wasn't too hard to see how he got his name.

He looked up at me and said, "Hey, man! What's happenin'?"

"Not much," I said. "How's it going with you?"

He was of medium height, natural brown curly hair. He seemed to be okay. Then I looked over at Lurch.

"So, wild man, did you get all those dishes sparkly clean?"

"Yeah, clean enough to eat off of," he laughed.

48

Lurch made the introductions. "So, Buddy, this is Son. Son, this is Buddy. He's the idiot I told you about that likes to work during the day."

I reached over to shake Son's hand. "Hey, somebody's got to do it," I said.

"Hey, Buddy," said Lurch. "Before I forget it… I ran a couple of those pills last night that you gave me."

"Oh, yeah," I said. "So what happened?"

"I got a little buzz off of them," he said. "But not much."

"Yeah, well, if you got a buzz off of two, then one would probably do for me. Look, guys, I got to get going. Nice to meet you, Son. How do you spell that anyway?"

"With an O," he replied. "S-O-N. It's not my real name."

I gave a chuckle. "Yeah, I sort of figured that. See you around!" Then I headed on back to the bedroom to finish getting dressed.

By this time Dawn was asleep on the bed. I decided that the best thing to do was just let her sleep. As I headed out the door, I was thinking it was really nice to have my car back again—bad brakes and all.

All right, I thought. *It's Friday!*

I had been invited to a party over at a female friend's house. Her name was Luanne. I decided that this weekend I wasn't going to feel any pain, and I definitely wasn't going to waste a single moment worrying about my questionable relationship.

CHAPTER 8

I went on to work and reported to Jake about the pills. We both agreed that we'd probably try a couple tonight. The day went pretty quickly up till about noon; after that, it seemed to sort of drag out. I'm sure that was because this was Friday, and I was ready to party. Man! Was I ready to party! The day finally ended. I grabbed my tools and my $103 paycheck and headed for the bank. I cashed my check, stopped by the liquor store, and bought a couple of sixes and a pack of Marlboros.

When I got home, I was happy to see that George was there, and he seemed happy to see me too—either that, or he really wanted a beer and I had one. We got to talking about our evening plans, and I suggested that he go with me to the party. He said it sounded good to him. He and Lora were sort of on the outs, and I knew he wasn't feeling really good about that. So we hung out for a while, talked, and drank a couple of beers together. Dawn and Lurch had already headed to work before I got there. George had already showered, so now it was my turn to clean up.

I was in my bedroom getting dressed, and he was doing the same in his room. While I was waiting for him, I took an old Pez candy dispenser and filled it with about a dozen of those pills. George eventually made it out to the living room, then off we went to Luanne's house—two guys, mad at their girlfriends, heading out to have some fun on a Friday night—or so I thought.

We stopped along the way at a 7-Eleven and bought a couple more six-packs and two bottles of Boone's Farm and a couple of bags of chips. We hadn't eaten anything yet. We made it to Luanne's house, and as we pulled in the driveway, I noticed there were already six cars there.

George started to get out, and I looked over at him and said, "Hey, wait just a second." I pulled out the Pez container, took two pills out, and swallowed them with the beer that I had just opened. He sort of squinted over to me.

"What was that?" he questioned.

"They are phenobarbitals," I answered. "Just a mild downer. You want a couple?"

"Uh…no, I think I'll just stick to my beer."

Once inside, we did the usual happy hellos. It was like, "Hey, Buddy, hey, George, what's happenin'?"

"How have you guys been?"

"You've been working?"

"Where's Lurch?"

"Where's Dawn?"

I answered everybody's question with one response—"Hey, yeah," and "I don't know!" At this, everyone went back to what they had been doing before we got there. Then around the corner came Luanne.

"Budman!" she said, and she came up and gave me a big hug.

She was originally from Georgia somewhere. She was short, had long brown hair, and was built like the proverbial brick outbuilding. Now why couldn't it have been her that I asked to move in? Make no mistake, she was no Snow White. She was just twenty years old and had already been married and divorced once. She knew her way around—now she could have lied to me about being divorced, and I don't think it would have mattered at all. I talked with her for a little while, then a friend of hers named Jo came up. Luanne introduced us. The three of us talked for a while, then the two of them walked off to "circulate," as they say. So I walked around, talked with some other people, ate some potato chips. Then I remembered the pills.

Those two pills that I had taken earlier had not done squat. They might as well have been aspirin. I would be embarrassed to give any of those away—well, maybe I should just take a couple more and give them a chance to work. Then Jo came back up to me and asked if I wanted to play a card game called "hearts."

She said sweetly, "You can be my partner?"

That made me wonder a little bit if her intentions were honorable. She then introduced me to the two organizers of the game, who turned out to be her cousins, Sam and Robbie. *Man*, I thought! *If we were playing for money, I'd be starting to get a little nervous right about now.*

About forty-five minutes later, I got to thinking about those pills. They sure seemed to be a bust! Four pills, and they hadn't done anything, but I figured they were probably out of my system by then, but I was curious to see what kind of a buzz Lurch was talking about. I excused myself and went to the bathroom. Four pills hadn't had much of an effect on me, so I decided to take three more. Then if that didn't work, I'd just forget about them.

I went back to the card game then, but somehow, eventually, it got harder and harder to concentrate on what I was doing. Now this game we were playing wasn't exactly rocket science, but after a while, I just couldn't seem to figure out what I was doing. What was that Jo was saying?

"Buddy, are you going to play or not?"

I just sort of stared at her, my head lolling.

"Buddy!" she said concernedly. "Are you all right?"

It was funny I hadn't noticed before what a hard game this was to play, and now her cousins were both staring at me with weird expressions.

Suddenly there was a flurry of confused conversation around me. I couldn't pick out who was speaking, but all of them sounded as if they were in some sort of echo chamber.

I heard them say, "I don't think he's all right…what did he take anyway?"

"Does anybody know?"

"Who'd he come with? Didn't he come in with George?"

Then suddenly George was there looking down at me with concern and disgust written all over his face. "Oh man! Those pills!"

He said something else too, and then the others said other things, but I was beyond even trying to understand what they were saying now. I vaguely realized that somebody was picking me up, and then I sort of checked out.

* * * * *

I don't know how long I was out, but I awoke to something cold and wet across my forehead. It felt good—but instinctively I reached up to push it aside; and as I did so, I opened my eyes to see—was that Kiki? She was bending over me, smiling her best angel of mercy smiles. It was so blurry I really couldn't be sure.

Still confused and very weak, I whispered, "Kiki, is that you? What's going on? What are you doing here?"

She gave a little gentle and relieved smile. "Nursing you back to health, freak!" Her voice had relief in it too. "And am I glad to see you coming around. Tell you what, I'll be right back. You just stay there."

As if I could do anything else at that point.

I lay there for a moment, then she came back with Lurch in tow, and I don't think I ever saw him looking so solemn as he did at that moment.

"You dumb son of a bitch!" he roared. "Don't you ever, I mean ever, pull anything like this on me again!"

I just lay there taking it. I certainly didn't have the strength to rebut.

"Your little LSD incident wasn't enough for you, was it? No... you had to overdose on phenos! Well, let me tell you something, man, if you're really all that interested in dying, do me a favor and do it the hell away from me!"

I'm sure he had a lot more to say, but Kiki took over then and grabbed him by the shoulder. "Okay," she said. "You've said your piece. Now just leave him alone." She led him out of the room then came back over to me and picked up my hand. "Don't let it bother you, babe," she said sort of stroking my hand. "He's just acting mad. You scared the hell out of him last night. For that matter, you scared the hell out of all of us." She stopped stroking my hand then and gave me a playful little punch. I started to chuckle.

"What!" she said. "What are you laughing at? It's not funny! It certainly wasn't funny last night! For a while there, we didn't know if you were going to make it or not."

She was right, but I had gotten a case of the giggles. "I'm not laughing at that," I said, and I noticed that my voice was a little stronger by now. "It's just that…well…that's the first time you've ever called me anything but freak." Meanwhile, I was still trying to sort things out in my mind. "But what's this about last night? What time is it anyway?"

She looked down at her watch. "Three seventeen."

I was confused. "But it's light out," I said.

She stared down at me. "Three seventeen in the afternoon," she said slowly. "You've been in dreamland like sixteen hours"—a mischievous little smile came over her face—"freak."

She then started to fill me in on some of the details: "While still at the party, George had recruited Sam and Robbie to help him carry me out to the car. Then after he got me home, he ran into the house screaming like a madman that you were out in the car and were really messed up. Some guys were here and helped Lurch carry you into the house. About halfway up the walk, you started barfing."

She looked at me then straight in the eye and said, "Lurch held you up when all the others backed off. Then he sent me for a clean rag to clean you up. Me and Lurch walked you around as best we could…you got sick three more times. Lurch figured that with all the throwing up you did, you'd probably be okay."

"So, you guys looked after me all night?" I asked.

Kiki nodded. "That's about the size of it, I guess."

Now something was bothering me, nibbling away at the back of my mind. "So…where was Dawn during all of this?"

She shrugged. "Your guess is as good as mine? She wasn't here when I came over last night—unless she's snuck in since I took Lurch back to the living room. She isn't here now either."

She left the room then, saying she'd let me rest for a while. I just lay back thinking how dumb and lucky I had been. I thought how if things had been just a little different, my mother could right now be sitting in some funeral home making arrangements. I honestly didn't know how she would have been able to handle this news if I hadn't pulled through especially from a drug overdose. I really wised up that weekend, and yet, a lot of parents have been through that—the late-night telephone call, the knock on the door. My mom had no idea what I was doing, and I suspect there are some parents that don't really know what's going on in the lives of their kids either—not until it's too late, that is. The worst part of it is the kids who have died of drug overdoses, and how many of them have there been through the years? They, for the most part, had no idea what they were doing either. Oh, I guess maybe some of them knew what they were doing, but very few. Like me, the vast majority of them probably just pushed the dosage up and up until they'd gone too far.

One thing was for sure. Either on purpose or by accident—once it's done, it's done!

CHAPTER 9

I spent the rest of that weekend on and off in bed. I did, however, muster up the strength to go to work on Monday. It wasn't until Thursday, though, that I really started feeling like my old self again. Was Lurch mad? Well, neither of us apologized to the other, if that's what you're wondering. Our friendship wasn't like that really. We didn't do much apologizing or worrying about that sort of thing. In time we just sort of grew back together, and things healed over. There was never any scar to be seen.

Son, by this time, had moved in with us. People just sort of drifted in and out of the house, and now we had three more bedrooms curtained off in the attic. The house had become a small commune of people.

As I lay in the bed that Saturday afternoon, I was still wondering what had happened to my girlfriend that Friday night and all day Saturday. It was finally about 6:00 p.m. when I heard her come through the front door, greeting everyone. I could hear her and Lurch talking, apparently about my adventure the night before.

I heard her gasp, "Oh my god! Is he okay? Where is he?" Seconds later, she's spraying into my bedroom, a concerned look on her face. "Buddy, what did you do?"

I told her the whole stupid story, and I promised her I would never do anything like that again. She had actually asked me to promise her that.

Then I changed the subject. "So, I was wondering where you were Friday night and most of today?"

"Oh," she said. "Lora and I were over at Granny's. You probably heard that she and George had a big fight, so I decided to stay with her." There was something about the way that she said those words that made me wonder if she was telling me the truth.

I finally decided it was time I let her know how I felt about our situation. "Listen, I need to get something off of my chest."

She looked at me really surprised.

"You know, when we first got together, I liked you. I enjoyed being with you. It seemed to me anyway that we were getting along pretty well. Maybe I couldn't really grasp at that point how one-sided this relationship would turn out. But I am beginning to see now, believe me. Did you really want to move in with me? Or did you just want to move into this house? I feel like I'm being used. I really don't like having this feeling. So you need to think really hard, and figure out if we are going to be together? Don't answer me yet…think it over first."

I got up to go to the bathroom, and as I did, I passed by George's bedroom door. It was open, and there was he and Lora lying in the bed and laughing with each other. So much for that lovers' quarrel. Apparently, they had gotten over their differences. It was nice to see. Just then, Lora looked up and saw me.

"Buddy!" she said as she jumped off the bed and came out into the hall to hug me. "Oh, Buddy! I was so worried about you last…"

I just sort of stared at her, "You were here?" I said incredulously. I certainly hadn't remembered her being there.

Now it was her turn to stare back at me. "Well, sure," she said. "Don't you remember?"

"I guess I don't," I told her. "I guess I don't remember much about last night."

Just a tiny fleeting look of hurt went across her face, then she smiled and hugged me once more. "I'm just glad you're okay."

I suppose I still wasn't thinking right because Dawn had just gotten through telling me that she and Lora were at Granny's last night. Now Lora tells me that she was at the house. The worst part was I didn't even realize that I had just been lied to. I went to the bathroom then headed back to my bed, and to my surprise, Dawn was still sitting there.

"Oh, Buddy," she said reproachfully. She gazed soulfully up at me. "Buddy, look. I'm sorry for the way I've been treating you. I guess I have been sort of thoughtless. I don't know… I've just been so busy at work and all."

I could see from the way she was sort of looking at me expectantly that she wanted me to interrupt, to say that it was okay. I decided not to say anything.

Finally, she continued, "I promise I'll come home every night right after work to be with you."

"That's good," I said, not believing a word of it. "Now, how about us getting some sleep?"

"Suits me just fine," she said, snuggling into my arms.

Nothing more was said.

* * * * *

I found it hard to believe, but over the next couple of weeks, things actually seemed to be working out between her and me. She was coming home right after work every night, and it really seemed as though she just wanted to be with me. We were starting to get close again, really close. I was lowering my guard more every day. Then after a week or so of this, I realized that my feelings for her were getting much deeper, which was something I surely hadn't ever counted on happening.

Back then I was always playing the tough guy, the macho man. I always acted as if nothing could ever hurt me or get through to me. If anything happened that should have bothered me, I just shrugged it off and said, "Oh well."

Now I could feel Dawn starting to penetrate that rough, tough exterior—and for once, I found myself sort of enjoying it. I found myself thinking maybe, just maybe, I finally found someone who really cares about me. Yeah, I thought Dawn and I had finally arrived—and then reality set in.

One day when I got home from work, Lurch was there, and he said that he had to talk with me. He had a strange look on his face, one that I had never seen before, so I knew just looking at him that it had to be something very serious.

"Sure!" I said. "What's up? Is the landlord pissed off at us again?"

"He probably is," replied Lurch. "But that's not what I want to talk to you about. Come on and sit down, man, I need to tell you something, but I'm not really sure how to do it?"

I did as he asked, and I have to admit that my heart was beginning to hammer a little as I did so. I had never seen him like this, and it scared me. I was beginning to wonder if maybe something had happened to my mom and he was trying to break it to me the best way he knew how.

I told him, "If you don't know how to say it, dude, just blurt it out! Can't be any worse than what I'm already thinking."

"Yeah, yeah, I guess so…" He was pacing back and forth now, which didn't add anything to my peace of mind. Finally, he turned to me, and it seemed as if the words were tumbling out of his mouth. "Buddy… Buddy, Dawn is cheating on you, man!" He stepped across and put his hand on my shoulder. "Look, I'm really sorry to have to be the one to tell you this. I just can't stand to see this crap going on any longer… You know I love you like a brother, man, and I just can't stand by and watch her make a fool out of you anymore."

I couldn't believe how serious he was, but for some reason, I knew there was no reason to doubt what he had just told me.

Meanwhile, I was dying inside. I just couldn't believe it at first. "How did you know about this?" I asked.

The word sort of caught in my throat. "Who's she…" I couldn't say what I started out to say. Then I caught my breath. "Who…is it? Do I know the guy?"

Lurch just sort of shook his head. "Are you sure you want to know?"

I took a deep breath. "Yeah," I said. "I think I need to."

"Okay," he said. "If you're sure about it." He began his pacing back and forth again. "Well, Jimmy and Vicky were down at Shakey's last week having some pizza. They saw Dawn's car pull into this Siesta motel across the street. They saw her and Son get out of the car and go into a room—room 20, Jimmy said. Jimmy said that he and Vicky were at Shakey's for at least an hour after that, and they never saw them come back out. So just for the hell of it, I approached Son and asked him if he and Dawn were at some hotel together. He actually admitted it. He said it was her idea and that she paid for the room. He said the first time that they went there was last Friday night—the night that you took those pills."

I was shaking my head in disbelief. So they went there twice I guess?"

Lurch nodded, "Yeah, I guess so."

At first, I wanted to pretend that I didn't just hear this from him. I wanted so badly just to shrug this off, to play the macho man again. For the first time in my life, I couldn't do that. I was at a complete loss for words. Never in my life have I had such an empty, hollow feeling inside. I felt stupid, betrayed, and embarrassed all at the same time.

One thing that I didn't feel, strangely enough, was anger at anyone—except myself, that is. One thought kept rolling over time and time again in my head. Dammit! I should've known! I should've known! I couldn't believe how mad I was at myself. But as for Son and Dawn, well, I guess I was still numb or something, but I really wasn't working up any anger against them—not then anyway.

Meanwhile, of course, Lurch was still sitting there, waiting anxiously to see how I was going to react.

I looked up at him, took a big deep breath, exhaled, then said, "Is there any beer in the fridge?"

Somehow I don't think that was what he was expecting me to say. He got this little half smile on his face, "Yeah," he said. "Yeah, there is. I'll get you one, man."

Do you know what the worst thing was? The worst thing was knowing that she'd be home in about seven hours or so. Ordinarily, I was looking forward all night to her coming home, but now—now somehow, I had to confront her, to let her know that I knew what had been going on. And how in the hell was I going to do that? I hated this! And what about Son, for that matter? How was I going to handle that part of it? This guy had been cozying up to me, pretending to be my friend, and all the time he was stabbing me in the back!

Meanwhile, Lurch was back from the kitchen, two beers in his hand. He had his full range of human feelings but could always be depended upon.

"So what are you going to do?" he asked.

I just shrugged. "I don't know, man. I've never been in this situation before. But I definitely have to do something. I need to confront Son too."

Lurch piped up. "Believe me, I'll take care of him."

"Well," I said. What I really feel like doing is going down to her work right now and having it out with her."

"Yeah," Lurch said soothingly. "I can see how you might feel that way, but you know you can't do that, don't you?"

"Why! Who's gonna stop me!" I bellowed.

He reared back in his chair a little and held his hand up, "Whoa now, man! Don't get mad at me. I just did you a favor, believe it or not." Then he seemed to settle down a little. "The reason you can't do that," he said patiently, explaining it to me as if I were a five-year-old, "is that it's a damn fool thing if you do it like that. You've got to handle this gracefully. If you go down there now all crazy and screaming at her, you'll just look like an idiot. Maybe they even call the cops on you, and you end up in jail." He took another sip of beer. "That's not the way to go, man! You've got to play this smart! Granted, you have to even the score…but stay cool while you're doing it! Make sure that when it's all said and done, you're the one who comes out of it looking good!"

It was like I was being briefed for a role on *Mission Impossible*. It did make me stop and think though.

"Yeah, I guess you're right," I said grudgingly, even though at that point I knew I had to do something, or my guts were going to explode. *How am I going to do that?* I thought. Even the score and still look good.

Lurch grinned at me. "Just think about it, man. I'm sure that you'll come up with a way. I've got faith in you."

I went out to the kitchen and threw away my empty can and grabbed another beer from the fridge and headed back toward my room to change out of my work clothes. As I was going through the living room, I noticed Lurch over by the front window. He was just standing there, looking down the street like a buzzard waiting for something to die.

"You waiting for somebody?" I said.

"Yeah, you might say that," he answered in a low, thick voice. "I'm waiting for Son."

"Isn't he at work?" I asked.

"Nope," he answered. "He's off today. He went over to his brother's house."

Then a little light went off in my head. "Wait a minute," I said. "How come you're not at work?"

"Oh," he said as he turned around to face me. "I guess I didn't tell you—I quit."

I was puzzled by that. I said, "I thought you liked that job?"

"Yeah, I did. Well… I don't know… I just couldn't stand being around that bitch anymore, I guess."

I just stood there for a few seconds, thinking about what he had said. Then I just said, "Oh," then headed back toward the bedroom. It looked a little strange because someone had closed the door, and I always left my bedroom door open. I was just putting my hand on the door knob when it hit me—the plan! My way of getting even with her. Oh yeah, this was beautiful! A broad evil smile spread over my face. "Yes!" I blared. Again, yes! It must have been pretty loud because Lurch came stumbling down the hall with an alarmed look on his face.

"What's going on man?" he said. "Why are you yelling yes?"

"I am yelling yes," I said, turning toward him with a grin on my face. "Because I know now how I'm going to even the score."

"How, man? How are you going to do it?" he asked.

"No, no," I replied. "No, you're just going to have to wait and see. Remember, patience is a virtue," I said sarcastically. "Once you see it, I think you'll be impressed."

I was on a mission now, and I was also beginning to feel a lot better about the whole thing now that I knew what I was going to do. I dressed quickly then headed on out the door and down the street to the neighborhood drug store. I bought some colored markers and a big white poster board and a roll of scotch tape. Next stop—across town to my mom's. She was surprised to see me.

We sat and chatted for a few minutes, then I got up and said, "I need to get something out of my old room."

It was a mess just as I had left it. I dug through the closet, and there it was—my old Mexican poncho that I picked up somewhere along the way, goodness knows where. I tried it on, checking the fit.

Yeah, I thought. *This will work!*

Walking back through the house, I said goodbye to my mom.

She said, "You're certainly in a good mood today. And why are you wearing that old…cape…for?"

"It's a poncho, Mom," I told her. "And yes, you're right, I am in a good mood right now, but it probably won't last." Then off I went.

Not too far from my mom's house lived a friend of mine named Saul. I hadn't seen him for a few months—but this really wasn't a social call anyway. He had something I needed, and I was sure that he would let me borrow it. He was home, all right, but he wouldn't let me borrow what I needed without an explanation. So I figured, oh well. I needed to tell somebody about my plan, and it might as well be him. So I told him the whole story about what had happened and what I planned to do about it. When I finished with my story, he just looked at me and grinned.

"You know what, man," he said. "You really are crazy!" Then he turned and took this huge Mexican sombrero off the hook that it was hanging on and handed it to me. "Here you go, man. Wear it in good health."

So out the door I went, headed for home. My plan was really beginning to come together. Now the only thing that could go wrong was if for some reason Dawn decided to come home early. I was definitely in a good mood now. Driving toward home, I bounced around on the seat, singing my own version of B. B. King's "The Thrill Is

Gone." Supplemented by a few choruses of "You done lost your good thing now"—referring to me, of course, as the good thing!

I was about a block away from the house when I saw Son walking in that direction, but I didn't stop. Like I said, he was only a block away, and I didn't feel like opening up that can of worms right now. It was really strange because, of course, I still didn't agree with what he had done to me—but I really didn't see any reason for me to be angry with him either. I mean if he really planned to stick around with Dawn, I figured he'd eventually get burned just the way I did. After all, that would probably be punishment enough—even though I knew Lurch had different plans for him. I got to the house before him and went inside to find George and Lurch sitting on the couch. You should have seen the look on their faces when I walked in wearing a poncho and carrying that huge sombrero in my hand. If ever there was an expression that said, "What in the world?"—that would have been it.

I looked at them and said in my best Leo Carrillo imitation, "Buenos Dias, amigos. Senior Son…he is approaching."

At that, they jumped to their feet and looked out the window. I was sort of anxious to see what Lurch was going to say to Son because I had already promised him, after all, that he could handle it. Then after he was done, I figured that I'd lay a little advice on him too.

I went into my room to lay my props on the bed when I heard Lurch saying meanly, "Here comes that son of a bitch!" I returned to the living room then and stood with George by the window as Lurch headed down the sidewalk toward Son on what was obviously by that time a collision course. I turned to George to ask him what he thought would happen.

Then Son greeted Lurch by waving a little peace sign at him and saying, "Hey, man."

Lurch raised his hand with an entirely different intent. Then *bam!* He pasted him, and Son fell down on one knee, holding his mouth. Now blood was starting to appear, and Son was completely dumbfounded. He looked at Lurch in horror.

"What are you doing? What are you doing?" he pleaded.

Lurch just stood there, his hand cocked and ready to give Son some more should he have that inclination. George and I were headed out the door at a trot. We didn't want to see Lurch hurt him anymore.

As I was coming down the steps, I glanced over toward the nursing home across the street. Man, you'd have thought they were having a fire drill over there. Those old folks were spilling out the door just as fast as they could hobble, and I heard a cracked old voice shouting out exultantly, "Fight! Fight!"

By the time George and I got out there, Lurch was telling Son to go into the house and get his stuff, that he was not welcome anymore. When Son saw me, he looked up at me. His lip was bleeding, I noticed.

"Hey, Buddy, I'm sorry man. I'm sorry," he said.

At that point, maybe he thought I was going to take a shot at him too, but I was actually feeling kind of sorry for him. Then he went on into the house to gather up his things while the three of us stood outside and the folks across the street looked on hopefully.

I turned to Lurch. "I didn't know you were going to split his lip."

"Hey," Lurch rumbled. "He's lucky that's all he got. I just don't know why I waited so long to do that."

Meanwhile, Son had gathered together his few articles of clothing in a box and was coming back out the door. He took one look at Lurch and decided to head off in the other direction, taking the long way home, and I really don't blame him given the expression on Lurch's face.

"Well," he said. "I suppose that's taken care of now. Let's go in and have a beer."

While we were having our brews inside, Lurch turned to me and said, "So, Buddy, what exactly do you have cooked up tonight for Dawn?"

"Oh, yeah," I said, sitting my beer down on the coffee table. "I guess I better get started on that, hadn't I." And I headed back toward my room.

"So aren't you gonna tell us?" said George, following me with his gaze.

"You'll see soon enough," I said, getting out my colored markers. "Hey, turn on the hallway light for me. I need more light for my masterpiece."

George did as I had asked, and I walked out into the hall, pulling my door shut behind me, standing there, markers in hand, sizing up the situation. Meanwhile, my roomies got up and came a little closer, taking in my every move.

I got out the tape and hung the poster board on my door first. At the top of the poster, sort of in a semi-circle, I wrote in various colors SIESTA MOTEL. As I did so, I was sort of half looking over at my admirers, and as I had anticipated, smiles were spreading over their faces. Then directly under the MOTEL sign, I wrote in slightly smaller letters ROOM 20. To the left of the room number, I drew a sombrero and to the right a picture of a cactus. Then underneath all that, I wrote the words WE RENT ROOMS BY THE HOUR. By this time, they were demanding that they were there when Dawn got home. I readily assented. Then on another piece of cardboard, I wrote the words NO VACANCY. I poked a hole in each side of that cardboard and ran a piece of string through the holes, creating a sign that I could wear around my neck. Then I put on the poncho and sombrero and sat down cross-legged under my masterpiece.

Lurch was beaming. "Oh, man, that's great. I'm proud of you!"

"Yeah," George said. "Do you know what? I almost feel sorry for her."

Lurch gave him a stern look.

Well, my trap was set. Now all I had to do was be sure to be awake when she got home, and revenge would be mine. By this time there were about four and a half hours to wait, and I'm sure you can understand me when I say that the clock just didn't seem to be turning fast enough. The funny thing was that my roomies seemed to be just about as restless as I was. We finally decided to order a pizza and play cards to pass the time. The only problem was we didn't have any cards in the house, so I headed down to the corner store to get cards and some more beer, of course, while they went to get the pizza.

The evening was moving right along now, and we were really having fun, laughing, joking, playing cards, and talking, maybe sometimes stretching the truth just a little. To tell you the truth, I had almost forgotten just how the evening had started.

Then suddenly it dawned on me. "Hey, what time is it anyway?" I asked.

Lurch looked down at his watch and said, "Damn, it's almost midnight!"

I pushed back from the table. "Go ahead and deal," I told him. "I'm gonna go and get ready. I'll be right back."

My actions were as good as my words. I went to my room and put on my poncho then got the sombrero and left it in the hall where I'd be sitting down when Dawn came in. Let's just keep playing cards until she comes," I said. "We can see her coming from here."

Those were brave words, all right, but I could feel the butterflies beginning to kick up in my stomach; and slowly but surely, my mind began drifting away from the cards in front of me to what I was going to say when she got here. After all, we were into the homestretch now. Like Lurch had said, I had to be cool and not act like a jerk. I glanced at the clock on the wall—twelve ten. I knew that she had to be on her way now, and there was no way that she could be suspecting this. I wonder what sort of a mood she would be in, how she would react when she walked in and saw me like that.

Wait a minute! What if she did know? After all, Son had left the house hours ago. What if he had gone down to the restaurant or had phoned her? Maybe she wouldn't even show up here at all. Maybe she was on her way to Granny's house right now instead of here.

Now I was really starting to sweat. What if I had gone into all of this elaborate charade for nothing? I wondered if I was the one who was going to be left with an egg on their face? Maybe I would have my revenge on her—or maybe she would end up burning me twice in the same night! *No! No!* I thought to myself. *Have a little faith man...have a little faith. It won't be that way—it can't be that way. It'll work out just the way you planned it. It's got to...it's just got to!*

Just then a pair of headlights came around the corner. I almost knocked over the chair, scrambling up out of my seat. That's her? I said, "It's her!"

Then the car we had spied went on down the street. I let out a big sigh and sat back down into my seat, my fingers now tapping on the table.

Lurch looked over to me anxiously. "Hey, man, take it easy!"

I just shook my head. "When the hell is she going to get here?"

Lurch, in turn, shook his head. "I don't know, man, but I do know that you've got to settle down. Don't sweat it! She'll be here soon enough. Just take it easy."

"I know, I know," I said. "It's just that…" And as I said the words, another set of headlights pulled around the corner, and this time it's slowed down and stopped. It was her. She was here finally.

It was showtime! Interestingly enough, I wasn't so panicky now.

Lurch looked over at me and grinned. "Okay man! It's time!"

I went to the hallway where I left the sombrero, slipped it on my head, and sat down in my pose. As I did so, I glanced down at myself to check my posture. *Damn, where is the sign? Where is my No Vacancy sign!*

I jumped to my feet, ran into my bedroom, and there it was, lying on the bed. It had been under the sombrero. Quickly I tried to put it on, but of course, it wouldn't go on over my hat. I jerked the sombrero off my head and hurriedly hung the sign around my neck and in my haste got it on backward. Muttering under my breath, I turned it around as quickly as I could, slapped the sombrero back onto my head, and scrambled out to the hallway. As I hunkered down again, I could hear Dawn coming through the door. Thank God I had gotten back in position in time!

Lurch and George, meanwhile, had positioned themselves on the couch, and I just hoped that the facial expressions they were wearing weren't giving anything away.

"Hi, guys," I heard Dawn ask. "Where's Buddy? In bed?"

"He's around…somewhere," Lurch said.

Then she turned the corner into the hall and stopped dead in her tracks when she saw me sitting there. "What the hell? Buddy, is that you? What's with the hat?" She looked down at the sign. "No vacancy? Have you guys all gone crazy or something? What is all this? What are you guys up to?"

Her feeble attempt at a joke didn't quite come across. Her voice was sort of thin and quivering. She looked back toward the living room. Is anyone going to tell me what's going on here? She waited for a moment and then when there was no answer from any of us just shook her head.

"You guys are nuts," she said. "So, what else is new?" Then she took a step over me toward the bedroom, and when she reached for the door handle, she stopped and looked at the graffiti. I could hear a little gasp that she gave and a muffled "oh my god!" Her hand flew up to her mouth, and she sort of leaned back against the wall as if her legs had just gotten a little weak.

She just stood there for a moment, staring at the doorway and the graffiti scribbled around it. I guess she was thinking through what she would do next, but I knew what to do. Standing up behind her, I took off the sombrero and the sign then lay them over on the couch. George, meanwhile, had a fascinating look on his face like someone watching a movie or something. I turned back to Dawn and saw that she was pointing toward the door.

"What's all this supposed to be, Buddy?" Was it my imagination, or did her voice sort of have a thin quivery tone to it?

"What does it mean?" I said. "Come on, Dawn!" I said, taking a step or two toward her. "Don't embarrass yourself any more than you already have, okay? Look, we both know what you did...the only problem is that you were the first to know it, and I was the last. I should have known better than to have gotten involved with you in the first place." I gave an ironic little laugh. "Come to think of it, I guess I probably did know, but I was just too stupid to care. Look, I'm done with you, and I am really done with all this. It's late, so you can come back tomorrow and get your stuff while I'm at work."

She was really starting to fume now. I could see the wheels going around in her head. She had to make one last-ditch effort to get back at me before she left, but the first thing she had to do was to position herself so that she could be center stage, as it were, so that everyone could see and hear her for her big scene. So she walked past me and out into the living room and dramatically turned to face me. "Well!" she spat at me. "Aren't we the Lord Bountiful all of a sudden! You're tossing me out on the street...but I don't have to move my stuff out tonight! Gee...thank you very much, you bastard!"

I was just about to really explode then, but Lurch must have known what was going through my mind because he caught my eye and gave a little shake of his head. I saw his lips forming one word—*no!* The whole idea behind this little presentation had been to get back at her but to leave me in a good light. To lose my temper now would just be to play into her hands. Meanwhile, she, seeing that her little ploy hadn't worked and perhaps seeing also how close that had come to work, pushed me—both literally and figuratively. "Do you want to know the truth, Buddy? Leaning toward me a little, she said the words: "The truth is that Son satisfied me. Do you understand? He's satisfied me—and that's something you were never able to do. So what do you think about that?"

I was really working on staying calm now. As a matter of fact, I let a few seconds go by before I started my reply. Counting to ten, I guess. "What do I think?" I repeated it slowly. "Okay, I'll tell you what I think. I think that you were satisfied, all right, but it wasn't Son who satisfied you. I think what satisfied you was lying and deceiving and cheating on me. Maybe that's all it takes to satisfy you. And... come to think of it, maybe that's really all that can satisfy you!"

She started to say something in reply, but I held my hand up in front of her face. I was on a roll now, and I didn't want to be distracted. "No, let me finish. I don't think that you're capable of having a normal relationship. And I'll tell you something else... I can see now why your husband dumped you! I guess what I really should be glad for is that I didn't reach that point with you. If I could find Son right now, I think I'd give him a big hug and thank him for what he did."

She just stood there now, staring at me. Once again, I could see the thoughts crowding through her brain, trying to organize themselves into words and sentences; but by that time, I think she had had enough of the whole thing. She stared over at me one last time—talk

70

about your hate stares—and then she concentrated all of her hate and frustration and viciousness into a single hate-laden word: "*Bastard!*" She flounced out the door, slamming it hard with a bang that surely must have woken up some of the tenants across the street. I turned to my audience, still sitting on the sofa, and they looked at me. There was a moment there, but all three of us just sort of stared at each other. Then they got up one at a time and raised their hands for a high five, and I gave it to them. Suddenly we all three were laughing and patting each other on the backs like we had just won the homecoming game. I think we were all very tired and glad that it was over. I know I was.

"Hey, you guys, thanks for the support… I really appreciate it," I said, suddenly feeling more tired than I could ever remember feeling before. "I've got to go to bed," I continued. "I am really beat." I went on into the bedroom, passed all that graffiti that I had painted over the doorway, and began to get ready for bed. I had forgotten that I was still wearing that old poncho. I pulled it off and threw it over in the corner—its task completed. I got into bed, sliding in between the sheets, and scrunched on over into the middle of the bed. I could sleep in the middle now that Dawn was gone. What a relief to have that twisted relationship behind me now! Her pillow was still there on the bed. I picked it up to throw it on the floor then decided not to do that. I caught the lingering scent of her perfume on that pillow. For some reason, I just had to smell that pillow once more before I threw it on the floor. Just like that, as if some evil sorcerer had waved a magic wand somewhere, all of the triumph and satisfaction I had been feeling just started to drain away. The pain and heartbreak I had been feeling earlier rushed in to fill the void. I knew right then that it wasn't going to be as easy as I had thought it would be getting over her. Once again, I picked up that pillow to throw it on the floor—but before I could do that, my arms just sort of took over for themselves and brought it close to my face so I could smell it again. Then I threw my own pillow on the floor, hugging hers against my head. Then I settled down for what I knew was going to be a long and lonely night.

CHAPTER 10

Those next couple of weeks seemed to stretch into eternity. This was, after all, my first real experience of heartbreak. To make it worse, I had been down to the Rocks a couple of times when she and Lora came in—and she always acted like everything was fine in her life, like breaking up with me was about as traumatic as stubbing her toe.

Why is that? Why is it that every time people break up, one of them is always down in the dumps and the other just carries on as if their life couldn't be better? I thought about that a lot in those first few weeks after the breakup. I came to the conclusion that in her case, it was because she would just never let on that a man had done anything to hurt her. I don't think that she was really all that tough inside. What it came down to, I think, is that she just didn't know what she wanted. I knew very much what I wanted though. What I wanted was to get rid of this sick feeling inside of me and get on with my life.

Meanwhile, things on the home front were getting pretty crazy. Our three-person household had expanded into a virtual commune. Vicky and Jimmy had moved in—you remember them as the couple who had seen Son and Dawn at the motel and had blown the whistle on them.

Jimmy was another childhood friend of mine whom I had met when we played Little League baseball together. We were on different teams, but we got to know each other pretty well. My memory of him in those years was him riding around on a bicycle with a banana seat and ape hanger handlebars. He rode around the neighborhood with his ball glove and his spiked shoes draped over the handlebars and his own bat over his shoulder. Sort of like gamblers, we were always looking for a game. Life was sure a lot simpler when I wore a baseball cap instead of a glazed expression.

So here was Jimmy, my buddy from my childhood, showing up on our doorstep with his current girlfriend, Vicky, one night and then deciding that the two of them should stay with us. Like I said before, it happened that way with us. We had a very informal sort of household. So now, George and I had the two bedrooms downstairs, Lurch had one end of the attic curtained off, and Jimmy and Vicky had the other end of the attic for their bedroom.

It's funny now looking back on those days. We weren't really any different from anyone else; we just somehow seemed to think that we had something to prove. Maybe it was our independence? We seemed to be very independent, just not very responsible. Let me give you an example. Five people were living there. The rent was $100 a month. The landlord paid the utilities. Now we were two months behind in the rent. Looking back at it now, if everyone could have just kicked in $10 a week, we would've had it made. The rent would have easily been paid. We would have had plenty of food and booze in the kitchen and maybe even a telephone? Only half of us had jobs, though, and even those who did weren't all that concerned about mundane things like paying bills. By the time the weekend was over and I bought lunch the rest of the week, it was all I could do to hold on until the eagle flew on payday.

There was one exception, however, a guy named Danny, who moved in with us later. Danny liked to party too, but he somehow seemed to think about things more seriously than the rest of us. Maybe that was because he'd just finished up a four-year tour with the Army. Anyway, one day Danny gathered us all together to make a speech about everybody pitching in so we could pay the rent. He made a nice little speech about how nobody should live here for free and everybody had to pay their share. He really stirred us up! His idea was to give our landlord some "good faith money," as he called it, to let him know we were serious about our obligations.

Danny passed the hat, and we came up with $60. Yes, that was a long way from what we owed, but at least it was a start, right?

"This is great!" Danny said to us. "I'm proud of you, guys, I really am. I'll give this to the landlord, and then every Friday will give him more until we're caught up. Let's make it a rule. If you can't pay your share, then you're out."

We all agreed. We were going to change things around, make a new start. We all felt good about Danny taking charge, and we were all glad we wouldn't have to face our angry landlord anymore. So he headed off with the $60 that we had collected, and we never saw Danny again—or the sixty bucks. Oh well, another lesson learned.

Then after Danny moved out, another guy moved in by the name of Chris—a tall skinny guy with flaming curly red hair with black Buddy Holly glasses. Chris's pride and joy was a five-foot-tall marijuana plant that he brought with him when he moved in. He was so proud of it. He put it up in the attic right next to his mattress so that he could keep an eye on it, which was probably not a bad idea with the kind of company that we had on a regular basis. It was almost a full-time job protecting it.

Chris also had a very distinctive way of driving. For some reason, he absolutely refused to sit through a red light if he could help it. No, he didn't run them. Instead, if he came up on an intersection where the light was turning red, he switched over to the right lane and turned. Then, of course, he'd have to work his way back to where he was going by turning again. I rode with him one time on a trip to the liquor store about ten blocks away, and I thought we would never get there!

One weekend when Chris was away, one of us—I don't really remember who it was—decided that his plant had been sitting around long enough! Its time had come! The thing about it was that the plant was still really green, and we didn't know quite how we were going to smoke it. Fortunately, though, we were in the company of Jimmy, also known as "Mr. Marijuana." We decided to put the matter into his capable hands, knowing that he could come up with some sort of solution. Sure enough, he did. It didn't take him long to discover that if one were to strip off a bunch of leaves and throw them into the toaster, the result was an almost instantaneous cloud of fragrance, shall we say. You know as well as I do that plant didn't stand a chance under those conditions. The worst part of it was adding insult to injury. We put the stripped-down plant back in Chris's room after we had pulled all the leaves off it.

What did Chris say when he came back, you ask? "How was it?" No, I don't think he liked it very much, and I don't think that he liked us very much either! I know this because he moved out the following weekend, and he took his plant with him! That was okay though. He was a little weird!

I guess the rapid increase that we were having in the number of tenants made George feel a little uneasy. Anyway, he announced one day that he was moving out. He found a small one-bedroom apartment just down the road from us in an old two-story house that was converted into two apartments. He would be on the first floor, and some other people we knew, Charlie and Marsha, lived upstairs. Charlie had somehow been tagged with the nickname Wimpy. Another example of a nickname hung on a person for no apparent reason. He played the harmonica, and he was really good, as I remember. Marsha was quite a bit older than he was, but it didn't seem to matter much to either of them or anyone else, for that matter, although she was definitely a lot more squared away than the rest of us. I guess that comes with age?

Anyway, I told George that I would help him move. So that coming Saturday, we loaded up his station wagon with all his earthly possessions, and off we went. Fortunately, his new pad was furnished, so he was set up pretty well. It wasn't long after that that Lora decided to move in with him. Talk about your shockers! Ken and Barbie living together? She still wasn't married, but at least now she got to play house. Obviously, she wasn't too comfortable with that situation, though, because it wasn't until she and George finally broke up a couple of months later that anybody even knew they were shacking up. That breakup would be the final one for them.

Well, now that George had moved out, we had an empty bedroom. Naturally, I wondered which of the attic dwellers would move downstairs. As it happened, none of them did. I guess they were more comfortable on the so-called second floor, away from all the foot traffic. So I was sitting in the living room one Saturday, mind-ing my own business, and there was a knock on the door. I thought this to be a little strange because once again, no one ever knocked on our door. I got up, opened it, and was relieved that it wasn't the landlord. What it was, however, was a young couple standing there, saying hello. They were holding two suitcases and a hopeful look on their faces.

I was just about to ask them who they were when the girl looked at me and asked, "Are you Buddy?"

"Yep, that's me," I answered. "Do I know you?"

"Oh, I'm sorry," he answered. "My name is Jack, and this is my wife, Gail."

Wow, I thought. *A married couple. We're really moving up.*

"Yeah, anyway, Buddy," he started in. "We were at the beach today, and we ran into this cat named Chris. We got to talking to him and asked him if he knew anywhere we could crash. He said you guys had this big attic, and some freaks were living up there. That sounded pretty good to us right now. We've been on the road almost two weeks, thumbing down from New Jersey. We always talked about coming to Florida, so I told Gail let's go."

"Oh yeah," I said. "Chris used to live here. Come on in, guys, and take a load off."

They came in and sat down on the couch, Gail leaning back against the cushions and closing her eyes. She looked like she was drifting off to sleep. She must've really been exhausted.

"I hope you don't mind," Jack said. "She's really tired."

Then I piped back up, "I think I've got some good news for you, guys."

"Good news?" asked Jack. "What kind of good news?"

"Well," I said. "As it so happens, we have a bedroom that's open right now. The attic dwellers said they didn't want it, so you're welcome to it."

Jack's face brightened. "Oh, man," he said. "That's great! Half an hour ago, we didn't know if we were gonna have a roof over our heads tonight. I was figuring on camping on the beach…and I really didn't like the idea of that. Then I figured we'd be sleeping on the floor up in some attic—if we were lucky—with at least a roof over us.

I led them back then to have a look at the vacant furnished bedroom that had once been occupied by George. Gail was ecstatic. It was so much fun to see her face light up! I guess sometimes it's the little pleasures in life that really matter the most. I mean—that bed had no sheets or blankets or pillows, and here she was going on and on about it. I thought about telling her that we had a hot shower too, but I didn't want her heart to give out. You know, too much excitement in one day—it's not good for a person.

"Look, Jack, you and your old lady make yourselves at home. Unpack and get comfortable, relax."

"Okay, Buddy." He nodded. "Thanks for everything, man! Really! Thank you!"

And then I went back out to the living room, and Jack and Gail presumably took a nap—a good long nap because I didn't see them again until noon the next day. I guess they were really knocked out. Hitchhiking all the way from New Jersey, wow! I used to hitchhike around town sometimes when I didn't have a car, but nothing like they had just done.

It's funny to think about how your life crosses the path of so many people—people you would not have known otherwise like Jack and Gail, for instance. They make it to Florida, they go to the beach and meet Chris; and the next thing you know, they're knocking on my front door. The best part of that was that I was able to help them out. I nor anyone else in the house had any misgivings, whatsoever, about taking them in and making them welcome. We knew nothing about them, but that just didn't seem to matter. Now the party just continued with two more participants.

Gail turned out to be really good at keeping the house cleaned up and actually doing some cooking. Jack went to work that next Tuesday morning at Lurch's old job at the box factory. After they had been there for a couple of weeks, it turned out that Jack's birthday was coming up. None of us knew this until one Wednesday afternoon when I walked into the house after work. I could smell something good cooking in the kitchen. Jimmy had pitched in and made a pan of cornbread. Gail and Vicky worked together to make a big pot of chili and a birthday cake for Jack? Then later that night, after everyone had gotten home, we all sat and shared in Jack's birthday dinner, after which Gail brought out the birthday cake, and yes, we actually sang "Happy Birthday" to him! We were turning into one big happy family.

So let's just count noses for a moment. Jack, Gail, and I were downstairs in the bedrooms. Lurch, Jimmy, and Vicky were up in the attic. We had just lost Chris and George, so we numbered six—however, that did not last for long. Lurch and I had been friends for a long time with a girl named Linda. Either one of us would do just about anything for her. So, when she had two of her cousins blow in from New York sort of unannounced, all she had to do was ask. Lurch told her they could make a room in the attic if they wanted to. Enter Joe and Phil from the Bronx.

Man, talk about your contrasts! These guys were as different from us as sugar is from salt. Lurch's hair was starting to get shoulder length, and mine was just plain long. Joe and Phil looked as though they were fresh off a *Westside Story* movie set—penny loafers, tight jeans with cuffs, short-sleeve T-shirts rolled up tight, ducktail haircuts, and don't spare the "groom and clean." We had never seen anything like them, and they could say the same about us. The cousins from New York had never smoked pot either—that is until after a couple of weeks with us.

I think that once upon a time I had probably looked like they did—somewhere around the fifth grade. I had finally talked my dad into letting me get away from the butch cut and let my hair grow out enough to slick it back. He let me do it, but he didn't like it much. Then when I got off the grease and let my hair grow long, he surely did not like that!

Check this out: Phil and Joe got a job right away—at McDonald's, no less! It was hard to think that someone living at the commune could get hired at a McDonald's. However, the fringe benefits were fabulous. I'm not talking about their fringe benefits; I'm talking about ours. Every night after work, they would come home with bags of food—yeah! I'm talking french fries, quarter pounders with cheese, fillet-o-fish—you name it, they had it. Was this a windfall or what? You can imagine what a tradition this became. Late at night some of us would be getting tired, but we weren't going anywhere until Phil and Joe got home with the goods. They usually got in around 11:00 p.m. One night I was getting kind of tired, and I actually asked Jimmy to wake me up when they got home.

"Are you kidding me?" he said. "No way, brother! You snooze… you lose, man!"

I don't think it was just the free eats that made those guys so popular, but that certainly didn't hurt them any.

So now there were eight of us living together in peace and harmony and McDonald's food wrappers. One thing about it, though, we had enough people living there now to have a party just by ourselves without inviting anyone else—not that we had ever invited anyone. People just always showed up. Having these people around was good for me during that particular phase of my life. I was getting to be my old freewheeling self again. The memory of Dawn was fading fast with the heavy partying I was doing.

CHAPTER 11

One night we were in the middle of one of those parties at the house when suddenly my eye caught sight of a girl that I hadn't seen before. She was sitting over on the couch with Jack and Gail. She was beautiful! I'm pretty sure that "Some Enchanted Evening" wasn't playing on the stereo at that moment, but it could have been. She had short platinum-blonde hair, beautiful blue eyes, a very slender figure, and a smile that made me weak in the knees. Lurch probably knew who she was, so I made my way over to him and asked about her. I asked him two questions: what was her name, and was she attached. As soon as I asked, Lurch's face curved up into a smile.

"Well, well, well!" he said. "Don't tell me you're getting interested in girls again, Buddy boy! Do me a favor—please don't ask her to move in with you."

"Don't worry, I won't," I said. "I just really want to meet her. What's her name?"

"Well," he replied. "Her name is Melissa. As far as being attached is concerned… I don't think she's secretly married if that's what you mean?"

Lurch's little joke went right over my head. All I knew was a beautiful girl had just walked into my life—or, at the very least, into my living room. Now all that remained was to make a connection with her. I didn't quite know how I was going to manage that, but I'd think of something. I was pretty good at improvisation, and how does that old saying go about necessity being the mother of invention?

So I walked by once, kind of slow, then stopped, backed up a step, then turned and looked down at her with a staged curious look on my face. She looked at me then, as I figured she had to, and my face broke out in a smile.

Curiously I asked, "I could be wrong, but I don't think I've seen you around here before?" Mentally I was thinking to myself, *If I had seen you before, I know I'd remember it!*

She gave me a tight little smile, trying to tell me, I think, that she knew I was hitting on her. "Actually this is my first time here," she said.

Her voice was just as beautiful as she was. Her smile opened up a little more, then oh, man! What a smile!

"And who are you?" she asked.

"Oh, I'm Buddy," I said softly. "And what's yours?" As if I didn't already know just as if, for that matter, she probably saw me talking to Lurch about her just a moment ago.

"I'm Melissa!" she replied, and then she continued after a short pause, "You live here, don't you?"

"Me? Yeah, I'm one of the originals."

Again, her lips twisted up into that mocking little smile. "Oh really? I don't think you're all that original, Buddy," she said. I'm sure she was referring to my courtship methods.

"So how did you know I lived here?" I inquired.

She sort of blushed. "Well, Lurch was sort of telling me about you before you got home tonight…but don't worry, he didn't say anything bad about you." She giggled a little.

I realized now that I was still standing there, my jaw hanging open with a sort of happy smile on my face. I must have been in some sort of a trance. That smile, that face, that little laugh had completely hypnotized me—then she delivered the knockout blow.

Staring back at me, she showed that dazzling smile of hers and said, "You're nice!" Then she slid over to the end of the couch and asked, 'Would you like to sit down?"

Wow! I thought. *Was this really happening, or was I just dreaming it all? Had this fair and gentle creature really asked me to sit down next to her?*

Jack and Gail were still sitting on the couch. When they heard what Melissa had asked me, they scooted over as far as they could, but there still wasn't much room.

Nevertheless, she patted the couch next to her and said, "Come on, now we've got room!"

So what could I do? I squeezed down between the two girls—a perfect fit!

Was I in hog heaven or what? Not only was I sitting next to this angel, but I was, as you can imagine, sitting real close to her; and of course, just to make a little more room, I threw my arms up around each of the girls and gave them a gentle squeeze.

"Well, now," I said. "Isn't this cozy?"

And boy was it ever. I was definitely enjoying this probably more than I should have been. At that moment, I felt that I was completely over what's her name? I guess it was true what they say—the only way to get over one relationship is to start another one. I'm here to tell you that it's definitely true. I hadn't felt this good in months.

After a while, Gail and Jack seemed to sense that maybe something was going on between Melissa and me. They quietly got up and moved into the kitchen. That, of course, left more room on the couch, but neither one of us seemed to mind that we were sitting so close together. We just sat there, talking about different things like music, other people that we knew, places we hung out—you know, the really important stuff. As it turned out, I knew her father. I had shot pool with him at a bar in St. Petersburg, but now I was wondering if I had made a mistake by telling her that. Then she asked if I had a cigarette.

"Oh, are you out? How about we cruise down to the 7-Eleven and get some?"

When we got outside, she asked me how far the store was. I told her it was only a few blocks away.

"Why don't we just walk instead?" she said.

Well, that was fine with me. As we started walking off down the street, her hand sort of naturally fell into mine. I honestly couldn't tell you whether or not my feet ever touched the ground. It was so simple, holding that hand in mine, so fresh and romantic and yet sort of awkward all at the same time. It was sort of like junior high all over again. We just sort of drifted along on our journey, talking in bits and pieces, enjoying each other's company. I was certain that I would never wash that hand again!

Finally, we meandered on back to the house; and instead of going back in, we decided to sit outside on the front step. Again we talked and talked, and while we talked. the party was sort of breaking up around us. I really didn't want this evening to end, but I knew that it was getting late.

"So Melissa?" I asked. "What have you got going on next Friday night?"

She looked over at me with a smile. "Nothing too important I don't think," she said. "Why?"

"Well," I stammered. "I'd really like to see you again if you'd like. Maybe I could pick you up, and we could go down to the 'Rocks' and listen to the band? *Please don't say no*, I was thinking. *Please, please, please!*

"Okay," she said, smiling. "I'll tell you what—I'll meet you over here after you get off work."

"Hey," I said, squeezing her hand in mine. "I'd be happy to pick you up?"

She gave a little shake of her head. "No," she said. "That's okay. I was coming over to see Lurch anyway."

Well, after all, she was his friend too. There wasn't any reason why she couldn't come over to see him. I was just happy at that point that she was willing to go out with me.

"Great! Then I'll meet you here," I exclaimed.

Then she responded softly. "Well, I suppose that I probably should be going." She turned a little more squarely toward me and smiled. "I really did enjoy your company tonight, Buddy. I'll be looking forward to Friday night."

Meanwhile, I was sitting there, facing her, just gazing into her blue eyes and listening to her words. Now I could feel the sweat gathering on my palms. I knew that the time was fast approaching when I would offer a kiss to end the evening. I figured that she would expect that. I mean, wouldn't she? After all, she had been kind of leading me on a good part of the evening. But, on the other hand, maybe she wouldn't. What if she didn't want a kiss on the first night that we met? This was crazy! Now I honestly didn't know what to do!

When she stood up to leave, I rose with her and said, "Come on, I'll walk you to your car."

Around the corner of the house, we went to where she had parked. I walked with her as far as I could, right up to the driver-side door. The butterflies were really starting to churn in my stomach now. We stopped, then she turned around and looked up at me.

"Well, I guess I'll see you Friday night then…"

I started to ease toward her. "Absolutely," I said in a quiet, slow rhythm. Then easy as that, our lips came together. All was right with the world now. She didn't pull away, and it was for sure that I wasn't about to. I could feel her warm breath on my cheek, and I could feel a heartbeat. The only thing was I didn't know if it was her heart or mine. Whichever it was, it was going mighty fast! All I knew was standing there with her in my arms was the only place in the world that I wanted to be. Kissing her was the only thing that I wanted to do.

We finally came apart, and I looked down into her eyes. She was blushing just slightly, and I suppose that I was too.

Then she gave another little shake of her head and whispered, "I really do have to go."

I smiled back at her and said, also in a whisper, "I know you do."

And then just like the other time, the words slowly grew into another kiss—this one a little shorter than the other one, I guess, but I had no complaints.

As our lips parted, I reluctantly thought that I'd better take charge. "Okay," I said. You really do have to get going now, young lady. I'll see you Friday!"

She smiled. "Umm," she said. "All right, I'll see you then." She looked to be just as reluctant to part with me as I was to have her go. She got in and started the engine. Several goodbyes and waves later, she was gone. I was missing her already! *Oh well*, I thought to myself. *I guess it's time to come back down to earth.* It was easier said than done.

As I went back up the sidewalk toward the front door, I couldn't remember the last time I had been that happy.

I pumped my fist in the air a couple of times and yelled, "Yes! Yes!"

I walked into the house and found Lurch sitting in his favorite green chair.

"Hey, where you been?"

"Out on the front step with Melissa," I answered.

"You two hit it off, huh?" he asked.

Grinning back at him, I said, "You might say that!"

Lurch gave a little shake of his head. "Just don't get in too deep this time," he barked. "You know what happened with Dawn?"

"Too late," I said, crossing toward my room. "I'm going to bed now to dream about her."

"Good night, lover boy!" I heard Lurch calling to me as I went around the corner.

"Good night, Mr. Wizard!" I shot back.

You know that I lay awake a good long while that night, replaying over and over again in my mind the night's events. I can't remember whether I dreamed about her or not, but I finally did drift off to sleep.

The next week, waiting for Friday to arrive seemed to drag on forever, but finally, the day had come. It began in the same old way—with the radio blaring on my alarm clock. However, the usual feeling of not wanting to get up had definitely left me that morning. This was, after all, the beginning of the day that would be followed by the night when I would once again be with Melissa—the girl for whom I was falling for much, much too quickly.

"Dummy," I chided to myself as I put on my clothes and headed for the shower. "Didn't you learn anything at all from Dawn?"

"No!" I answered myself, a great big happy smile on my face as I chuckled to myself. "No, I guess I didn't."

For once in a long while, I had a spring in my step as I walked out the door to face the day. When I walked back in the door, I thought, *She'll be here. She will be here!* I even made it to work about twenty minutes early that day—believe it or not. I know my boss had trouble believing it! I was in a great mood and nobody knew why and nobody asked even though I was more than willing to tell them why I was feeling so good!

The day was going by pretty quickly until the last hour or so. I was so excited about seeing her again I just wanted this day to end. I found myself wondering about her—you know, what was she doing right now. She hadn't told me where she worked or if she did work, for that matter. I wondered if she was thinking about me, if she was as excited about tonight as I was. I sure hoped that she was.

The day finally ended, and off I went like a shot to the bank, my paycheck in hand. As I was coming out of the bank, I noticed a girl a couple of doors down that was selling flowers. That sort of seemed to fit right in with the scheme of things—you know what I mean?

I went right over to her and bought a white rose to give to Melissa. The girl looked at me, thanked me, and said, "God bless you, sir!" I had never been called "sir" in my young life. I had no intention of being called sir for some years to come, I thought. I seemed to have missed the part about God blessing me. Anyway, with a week's pay in my pocket and stars in my eyes, I hopped into my car and headed on down to the liquor store. I bought my usual two six-packs and then decided to buy a bottle of Boone's Farm for Melissa. Everyone that I knew had been drinking that stuff for a while now. I hadn't even been out with her yet, and I had already blown five bucks on her. Maybe she was too expensive for me? I laughed.

Now I was headed home. I wasn't quite sure exactly what time she'd be there, but I figured that if she hadn't shown up for a while after I showered and changed, I could just while away the time chatting with the inmates until she arrived. I opened one of the beers and sort of nursed on it as I went, singing along with the radio and completely contented with where my day was heading. Then when I turned onto the street our house was on, I looked around the corner, and there was Melissa's car sitting at the curb by the house.

Boy! I thought jokingly. *Is that a girl who is anxious to see me or what?* I got out of the car with my beer and wine in hand but left the rose there on the front seat. I thought I'd just give it to her later; I didn't want to give it to her in front of everybody. I didn't want to be teased about it later. I jumped up the front steps, two at a time, and crossed the front porch. As I entered the house, I was a little puzzled. What was this? No music? There was never a time when people were home that there wasn't some music playing. I wondered if anybody was here. Her car was out front. I wondered where they were.

I headed for the kitchen to put my package in the fridge. I heard a little muffled talking coming from behind the kitchen door. Then peering a little more closely into the room, I could see Lurch and Melissa sitting close together at one corner of the kitchen table. He was holding one of her hands like maybe he was pulling on a splinter.

"Oh!" I called cheerily. "So there is someone home? I didn't hear any music when I walked in, so naturally, I assumed—"

"Shhh," hissed Lurch. "I'm trying to concentrate!"

I was leaning over Melissa's shoulder by this time, and I could see it all. As I'd seen from across the room, Lurch had hold of her hand with one of his hands, and the other held something that I had not expected. He had a hypodermic needle in his hand, and he was pushing it into her arm.

"Oh my god," I said softly. A queasy feeling started turning in my stomach. I went to the refrigerator to put my package away, and when I turned, I was staring right at Melissa's face. She was pale, and she had broken into a sweat. The worst part was that it didn't even look like her. There was an awful blank stare on her face. I was looking right into her eyes now, and she didn't even see me. Then she raised her head slightly and looked at me, but it still didn't seem like she even saw me. This can't be happening! This was not the girl that I liked so much just last week. I was in shock. I just couldn't believe that this was happening!

With my heart in my throat, I turned and groped my way to my room; and for the first time ever, I shut the door. I felt tears coming to my eyes—which was not the usual occurrence for me. I turned around and locked the door. I didn't want anyone to see me like this. Through it all, I was thinking, *How can this be happening to me?* Ten minutes ago I was on top of the world—and now, God! How quickly things can change. My lips curved up briefly in a bitter smile.

Well, I thought. *I guess now I know why she was coming over to see Lurch...*

Just then there was a rattle on the doorknob. "Hey, Buddy," came Lurch's voice from the other side of the door. "Hey, man, are you in there?"

Even in the state of mind I was in, I couldn't help noticing the absurdity of that question. I suppose there wasn't much else he could say, thinking back on it. I'm sure the fact that my door was closed and locked must have really shaken him up.

I shouted back at him, "Who do you think is in here?" My voice was shaking both from crying and from my anger. I was furious at him right now!

"Hey, Buddy, let me in, man!" he pleaded. "I hate talking through doors!"

I hesitated for a moment. I really wished that he would just go away, but I knew that he wouldn't and that I would have to talk to him. *I should have just headed back out the front door when I saw what was going on*, I thought bitterly. Of course, with the state of mind that I had been in right then, it may not have been a good idea.

"All right," I called back to him resignedly. I went across the room, opened the door, and let him in. In he came with a deep look of concern on his gaunt face. I gave a little wave of my hand toward the bed, and he sat down. Then I let him have it with both barrels.

"So, just what the hell do you think you were doing to her out there? I suppose that was your idea—you and you're damned needles!"

"What are you talking about?" he roared back. "It wasn't my idea. It was hers all the way. I was just helping her out, man!"

"Helping her out!" I screamed, pounding my hand down on top of the dresser so hard that it hurt. "Helping her out? Shooting her full of that...whatever it was. Yeah, you sure have a funny way of helping people out!"

Lurch just stared up at me. Now speaking a little softer, he said, "Buddy, can't you see what she is? She's a junkie, man. Her boyfriend used to do it for her, but they broke up, and she asked me if I could help her."

I stared across the room at him. "A junkie? No way, man, she can't be…not her? She's so sweet," I choked out.

"Well," he answered back. "You do like her, don't you?"

"Yeah! I do. I mean I did, but that's before I knew what she was. I can't do this, Lurch, I just can't!"

Lurch stood up, reached out his arm, and patted me on the shoulder. "Hey, man, I'm really sorry, I am. I know how hard this must be for you…that's why I said what I did last night to you, remember…about not falling too fast for her? Maybe I should have told you a little more about her last night, but you just seemed to be so interested in her. I thought it might be good for both of you."

Then I told him, "Sorry, dude, but I just can't do this. I'll always wonder which Melissa likes me. I'm outta here!"

Lurch then stood in front of me. "What about Melissa? I thought you two had a date?"

"Yeah," I said. "We did, but now I guess we don't! Just tell her something came up and I had to leave, and I had to get out of here!"

"She was really looking forward to it," he said. "She told me she was."

"Yeah," I said as I headed for the door. "So was I!"

Out to my car, I went. I started her up and roared on down the street, all sorts of thoughts swirling in my brain. I suppose that it must have been another of those instances of the Lord looking after me? I probably wasn't fit to be driving a car the way I was feeling right then. I had no idea in the world where I was even going. I knew that I had to get out of there as soon as possible. Any place else would do far as I was concerned. I was boiling over, mad at the world and brokenhearted again. One thing was for sure—my feelings about the opposite sex were changing rapidly. I certainly had to change the way my relationship with girls was going. Was it her fault that I felt this way, or was I just overreacting? Why didn't she tell me of her addiction? Then some other part of my brain laughed back at me. Oh, yeah, sure, that's going to happen—happens all the time right! "Hello, my name is Melissa, and I am a junkie. Does that bother you? If not, maybe we could go out together sometime?" Get real!

Then I began wondering about how she felt about doing heroin: did she enjoy it, hate it, or just put up with it? I thought it could have been so nice for her and me if she felt about me the same way I felt about her. All of these thoughts kept rolling through my head when all of a sudden, I realized I was in my old neighborhood.

I thought, *Well, if I needed some place to go to calm down, it would certainly be at Mom's. Maybe I could get away from all this insanity for a while.*

I pulled into the drive and parked, and as I did so, I noticed that rose I had bought for Melissa. It was still sitting on the front seat. A smile came over my face and I thought to myself, *I know who really deserves this.* I reached over for the rose and picked it up and slowly got out of the car and went up the front walk. As I entered the door, I could see mom sitting at the dining room table, sorting some papers. She looked up at me then; a warm mother's smile took shape on her face. I walked over to where she was sitting and grinned back at her. I held the flower out toward her.

"Here you go, Mom," I said. "This is for you."

CHAPTER 12

My mother had been at the table, sorting through papers for her Sunday school lesson. She had taught Sunday school for over fifty years before she retired and handed the reins to someone else. She wasn't a college graduate; she had no degree. What she had done all of her life was just work hard for her family. She and Dad did the best that they could for us.

She could see right through me, and she asked me if something was wrong. I really didn't want to tell her what had happened to me. She told me to sit down and she would get me a glass of iced tea. I figured this iced tea would be safe to drink. She came back from the kitchen and set the glass in front of me.

"So what brings you over here today?" she asked.

I decided it was time to confide in her. "Well, Mom, last week I met a really nice girl. As it turned out, she wasn't so nice, and I really liked her."

She slowly shook her head back and forth. "Oh, I'm sorry to hear that, Bud." "What happened?" she asked.

I knew I couldn't tell her the truth, so I just said, "It just didn't work out the way I thought it would."

"You know, Bud," she said. "There are a lot of nice girls at the church your age. I really wish you would start coming back to church with me again on Sundays."

I had been going to church ever since I was born as I can remember it. We went to church every Sunday when we lived in Ohio, and now again in Florida—the Southside Baptist Church. I had sung in the junior choir there. I was baptized there when I was twelve years old along with some of my friends. I remember I tried to hold my nose on the way down, but my hand slipped off, and I came up with a nose full of water. I was coughing and choking while the rest of the congregation was applauding. My mom asked me later if I felt any different. I told her, "I don't ever remember being that close to drowning."

My father had attended church as a young man; that's where he and my mother met. There was twelve years' difference in their ages. My father had polio as a teenager, and now because of that polio, one of his legs was shorter than the other. My dad would go to church with us maybe twice a year now. I learned later in life that when he and my mother had decided to get married, the preacher of the church told my mom that my dad would never be able to support her and a family because he was a cripple. I guess at some point my father found out about what he had said, and he never went back to church again. He truly believed that the church was nothing but a bunch of hypocrites.

One Sunday when we arrived at church, we got some shocking news. Apparently, our preacher and our choir director had fallen in love and decided to run off together. They were both married with two children apiece. Well, that was all my dad needed to hear. Talk about adding fuel to the fire!

I stayed at my mom's for a couple of hours that afternoon, just sort of talking things over with her. Talking with my mom always had a calming effect on me. We just sat and talked about friends, family, and how my job was going.

I didn't know it at the time, but things in my life were about to take a turn in a different direction. My dad had been dead for a few years now, and my mother was sharing the house with one of my sisters and her three kids. My sister was going to be moving out to live with her boyfriend. Mom would be moving in with my youngest sister and my brother-in-law in their new home. That meant the house would be empty. She said if I wanted to, I could take over the house—the payments were only $60 a month. The only trouble with that was $60 was a lot of money to me back then plus the utilities. I knew with my $103 paycheck every week that I could swing it, but that would take up a lot of my party money.

"Well," she said. "Your cousin Bob said he might be interested in taking it over. Maybe the two of you could share expenses. If that doesn't work out for you, then I'll just turn it over to the lady that we were buying it from."

"Oh no!" I said. "You can't just give it back. There can't be that much more owed on it, can there?"

"Well," she said. If you feel that way, you and Bob should get together and discuss it. Either way, I'm leaving."

Actually, the more I thought about rooming with my cousin, the more it seemed that it might work out. He and I were really kindred spirits—we both liked to party. In fact, he told me once that the only difference between him and I was eighteen years. I hadn't seen him in a while, and we did always get along pretty well, I thought. I decided I would check this out.

Suddenly I looked up at the clock, and it was seven fifty already. I decided I better go and check out what the gang was doing up Gulfport way. I said my goodbyes and headed for the door. Mom thanked me for the rose again and reminded me that I didn't have to stay away so long.

I answered, "Yeah, Mom, I know," and then she ended the conversation as she always did: "I'll be praying for you, Bud!"

I jumped into the car and started it up. This old car was amazing! It always started! Sometimes I had trouble stopping it, but it always seemed to start. I slipped it into drive and pulled out onto the street then stopping at the stop sign. As I was sitting there, watching for cars, a feeling of uncertainty hit me.

I said to myself, "So where should I go? Should I go to the Rocks, or should I go back to the house? If I went back to the house, Melissa would probably still be there, and that probably wouldn't be a good thing for me. I wondered if she had even known that I was there in the first place in the condition that she had been in. The image of her sitting there with that needle in her arm was going to haunt me for a long time. What would she think of me now that I had walked out and stood her up? One thing was for sure—I couldn't sit at the stop sign all night.

I decided to head to the Rocks. Now I began formulating a more definite game plan. I'd cruise by the bar, and when I got there, I could circle around a couple of times and look for her car or the red Volkswagen that Lurch just bought. If they weren't there, I would stop in. If they were, I would just go back home and party with the inmates.

On my way, I passed Saul's house, the guy I had borrowed the sombrero from. He must be starting to wonder how long I was going to keep that thing. I decided I would take it back to him for sure tomorrow. That was tomorrow. Right now, I was on my way to the bar to start my weekend all over again. I could just taste that first cold draft beer going down. When I arrived, I circled the bar a couple of times and didn't see any sign of Lurch or Melissa. I parked the car and headed for the door, and as I entered, I could hear the jukebox playing "Bennie and the Jets" by Elton John. It had gotten to the point in the song where Elton sang out, "Benny! Benny!" But this time, somebody inside was singing, "Buddy! Buddy!" in my honor. I looked around to see that it had been Luanne that was singing. She and Jo were sitting at a table along with Jimmy and Vicky.

Luanne jumped up enthusiastically; I guess she was in a hugging mood that night. "Buddy!" she slurred, squeezing me tighter. "Give me a hug! I need a hug tonight!"

I obliged her, of course, looking over her shoulder at Jo as I did so. "So what's happening with you tonight?"

She had a tired smile on her face and gave a little shake with her head. "I'm getting ready to take her home. She's been here since three this afternoon."

I grinned. "Yeah, she doesn't seem to be feeling any pain."

"You have to excuse her. She found out today that she's probably going to lose her house...so she's...celebrating, I guess?"

About that time, I noticed Jimmy was trying to get my attention.

"Hey, Jo," I said. "Let me know what happens with her house? She could always come and live with me." *Oh, Lord*, I thought. *Did I just do that again?*

Jo looked at me absurdly. "Right, I'll let her know."

Well, now I was looking over at Jimmy. "What's happening, my friend?" I said, giving him the seventies handshake.

"Hey, Bud," he replied. "Lurch and some chick were in here looking for you, man. They were here maybe…oh, about a half hour ago. So where have you been tonight?" he asked.

"Oh, I stopped over at my mom's," I answered him.

"Wow," said Jimmy in a reminiscent tone. "Man, I haven't seen her for a long time…how she doing anyway?"

Vicky's jaw dropped. "You know Buddy's mom?"

"Oh yeah," Jimmy said. "Me and Buddy go way back, don't we Bud? We grew up together."

Long about then, I felt a light tap on my shoulder; and turning, whom should I see but Lora standing there. She was smiling her little Barbie doll smile.

"Lora," I said. "Good to see you."

Lora's smile brightened a little, and then she looked down as solemn as I've ever seen her look. "Buddy," she said. "Is it okay if you and I talked for a moment?"

"Sure," I said. "What's on your mind, sweetheart?"

Her smile flashed again. "Oh, nothing really, just a moment of your time. Can we sit over there in the back?"

"Sure," I said, feeling puzzled at what she wanted to talk to me about. Then I realized I still hadn't gotten a beer. "Lora, if you can wait a couple of minutes, I want to go get a beer. I'll meet you back at that table."

It took a few minutes, but true to my word, I got my drink and met her toward the back of the bar. She didn't seem to be upset, so I sat myself down at the table and asked, "So what's on your mind?"

"I don't know. I just…haven't seen you for a while. I was wondering how you've been doing is all."

I looked sharply over at her. She could've asked me how I was doing over at the other table. I figured she probably had something more important on her mind than the state of my health. I figured there was no sense rushing her though. She'd get to the point sooner or later. Meanwhile, I was enjoying her company.

"Well… I'm fine. So how are you?"

She shrugged. "Oh… I'm okay, I guess… Buddy, I'm over George…"

This wasn't exactly a hot conversation we were having here, but I was determined to be patient.

"Yeah, I heard that you two broke up. I'm glad that you're not, well, grieving about it," I said with a grin.

It was obvious that she was groping for words or for the way to say those words. Finally, I could see it on her face as she did it. She resolved to take the bull by the horns. "Buddy…are you over Dawn?"

I hesitated a few seconds before replying. I was still trying to figure out just where this conversation was headed. When I did speak, it was with confidence. "Well, sure, I'm over her," I said. "Heck, I've gone with and broken up with another girl since then!"

Her eyes got real big. "You have?" she said in a shocked tone of voice then sort of tilted her head as if she wasn't quite sure whether to believe me or not.

"Oh, yeah, girl," I said with a half-joking tone of voice. "You know me, I go through women almost as fast as I go through beer." I smiled at her."

Lora drew a long, slow breath. "Well, Buddy… Dawn's not over you yet. She's still a little heartbroken about what happened between you two."

"Oh, bull!" I said, probably a little too strong. "She's not heartbroken! She was over me the same day we met, and that's the gospel truth!" I looked sharply over at her. "Just what are you doing anyway, Lora? Why are you getting yourself involved in this? Did she put you up to this?"

"Look, Buddy," she said, leaning across the table toward me a little bit. All she really wants is just a chance to talk with you. She's really trying awfully hard to get her life together."

I just sat there, shaking my head. It seemed to me that I'd heard that line before, I thought—except that she never used the word *life*.

"Look, sweetie," I said with a little sigh, trying to regain my composure. "Listen, I'm sorry if I snapped at you. I didn't mean to… but believe me, you're getting in way over your head on this one. Just for the record, let me say it... I have absolutely nothing to say to your sister. Nothing. Zilch!"

"Well," she said, looking sort of discouraged. "If you should change your mind...she's sitting down there at the end of the bar."

A hot wave of anger swept through me. I'd been had! Clearly now, Dawn had to put her up to this! "Look," I said. "I gotta go!" Suddenly, it was all that I could do not to look down at the end of the bar. I knew damn well that Dawn was looking over at us!

"Are you going to talk to her, Buddy?" Lora asked in a last-ditch effort.

I looked down at her witheringly, swigging the last of my beer and setting the glass down on the table. "No... I am not going to talk to her," I said heatedly. "You tell your sister for me...just...just don't tell her anything. She's out of my life now. You can tell her that!"

That being said, I headed hastily toward the door, not saying goodbye to anyone.

As I started up the car and headed out of the parking lot, I wondered for a minute if Lora had ever known what had happened between her sister and me. After all, she had probably not gotten the true story from Dawn. Somehow I couldn't imagine her telling her sister the whole truth. If she had told her anything, I'm sure she would have spun it in her own version. She probably just told her that I threw her out because I was a—as she had put it—a bastard!

One thing was for sure—this weekend was not even vaguely in the competition as one of my better ones. But as I turned toward home, one ray of sunshine gleamed on the horizon. As I thought about it, a smile came gradually back to my face. Yes! Maybe there was hope for me after all. Maybe things could change; maybe they could get better. Now I was convinced I was in control of my own fate, the master of my destiny, captain of my soul. That might be a little much—all I had to do now was make it home in time for my rendezvous with Joe and Phil and all the McDonald's leftovers! This always put a smile on my face! So I pulled out and headed for home.

Then as I was about half a mile from my house, my eyes opened wide—I couldn't believe it! Was that a New York plate on the car in front of me? It was the hand of fate, no doubt about it. My weekend had definitely taken a turn for the better. Unless I was very much mistaken, that was Joe and Phil's car, right in front of me! Probably sitting on the backseat were bags of goodies—Big Macs, quarter pounders, fries, and sometimes even filet-o-fish sandwiches! I hadn't had anything to eat since lunch, so my mouth was watering right now.

I'll have the first pick tonight! I thought exultantly. *I'll hit 'em up before they ever get inside. Nothing like a couple of quarter pounders to sort of put your life back into perspective.*

Finally, we both pulled up to the curb at the same time, with me right behind them. I turned off the lights and the engine and got out and casually walked over to the car. As I walked toward their car, I noticed a body staring out the window of the house. It was Oh Dammit No Anthony!

Anthony—not Tony—because he would not let anyone call him Tony! None of us really liked him that much. He was pretty full of himself. He started showing up on the weekends sometimes. He would bring some of his own records and force us to listen to them— kind of a bossy person.

One evening, Lurch saw him coming around the corner of our house and blurted out, "Oh, dammit no, Anthony!"

From then on, that became his name. Later on, we just shortened it to Oh Dammit No!

Anyway, it was Anthony that was staring out the window. He was a Big Mac fanatic. I knew he was patiently waiting to see if there was a Big Mac in one of those bags. As I said before, I didn't like him all that much, so now I had an idea. Meanwhile, Joe and Phil were getting out of the car, walking toward the house. I intercepted them.

We greeted each other, and then I asked, "Do you have any Big Macs tonight?"

Phil said, "Yeah, but only one." He dug through one of the bags and handed me the sandwich. "Here you go," he said.

As the three of us proceeded toward the house, I took the burger out of its container and started gnawing on it immediately. As we walked into the house, it was easy to see who had the munchies. Not only from the red eyes but also by their mouths watering at the smell of all that McDonald's aroma waffling through the house. Anthony's eyes were red as usual, and I just knew what he was going to look for. He had the air of a man on a mission as he looked frantically through those bags, trying to sniff out his beloved Big Mac.

Finally, he looked up at Joe in desperation. "Joe, aren't there any Big Macs tonight?"

Joe answered him, "We had one, but Buddy beat you to it!"

Anthony looked at me as if I had just shot his dog. He just stared at me in horror and groaned, "Buddy! You took the Big Mac?"

In the meantime, I had sat down in the green chair to finish my late-night snack. My mouth was so full I couldn't reply. I just nodded. "But...you don't even like Big Macs! You like quarter pounders!" Just to rub a little more salt in the wound, I licked my fingers, giving each of them a loud smack! "Anthony," I said, pausing to pick up my napkin and properly clean my lips. "I'll tell you this much... I certainly enjoyed that one!" Then after just the right amount of pause, I added, "I heard someone say once—if you snooze, you lose. Is that true?"

With a great deal more noise and fuss than was really necessary, Anthony rooted noisily through the bags as he pulled out a quarter pounder. I decided it was time to add the finishing touch.

"Hey, Anthony..." I said in my most reasonable tone of voice. "If it'll make you feel any better, you can put your quarter pounder here in this Big Mac carton—"

"And you can go to hell!" he said venomously as he slipped on out to the kitchen.

I was shocked! I mean, after all, he made it sound like I took that Big Mac on purpose! Geez! I was really never that mean to people, but like I told you before, I really didn't like this guy. Or maybe I was still upset because of the way my weekend started?

Just then the front door opened, and in came Lurch. He seemed to be in an awful hurry. I figured he just wanted to get some food before it all disappeared, but then he walked straight up to me and pointed his bony finger.

"You! And where the hell have you been all night? I've been looking everywhere for you!"

"That's why you didn't find me," I said in my best smart-aleck fashion. "I haven't been everywhere. But then again, I guess you did find me—and right here where I live too…which just goes to show what an excellent job of stalking me you did!"

"Aren't you the smart ass tonight!" he fired back. "Seriously, though, where were you?"

"I was at the Rocks," I answered.

"Who are you trying to kid?" demanded Lurch. "I know you weren't there. Me and Melissa were there looking for you!"

"Yeah, I know you did," I replied. "Jimmy told me all about it. I was at the Rocks later after you guys left… I stopped off at my mom's first."

"Listen, man," he said. "We need to talk, so let's go back to your room."

I gave a little nod of approval. "Okay, I'll meet you there. I'm gonna grab us a couple of beers." With that, I got up and went to the fridge; but when I opened the door, what should I see? A very familiar-looking brown bag sitting on the shelf. *No, it can't be*, I thought. I set the beer on the table then reached back in for the bag. I opened it and looked inside. Sure enough, there it was—my precious bottle of Boone's Farm wine I had bought earlier. Considering our household, this was pretty remarkable! Grabbing the beers and bottle of wine, I headed back to my room. Lurch was there sitting on the bed, patiently waiting for his beer. I sort of backed into the room, hiding the bottle of wine in front of me. I handed him his beer and then revealed—"Tada…the Boone's Farm."

"All right!" He popped the tab of his beer and took a long drink. I put the wine bottle down on the nightstand.

"So," he said, sort of leaning back and looking into my eyes. "Are you all right with Melissa?"

It struck me as sort of a strange question, but then again, I suppose that he had to open the conversation up somehow.

"Am I all right with Melissa?" I repeated. "Sure, I'm all right, I guess—except I'm not with her, am I? I'm sitting here with you instead! So does that mean that I'm all right with her or all right without her…or just all right period?"

Now it was his turn to be confused. He looked back at me with a slight tilt to his head. "Well," he said slowly. "I guess it means that you're okay, but Melissa is not okay."

I cracked open the bottle of wine and handed it to him. He took a big swig and then handed it back to me.

He looked at me and said, "She told me to tell you she was sorry!"

"Look, man," I replied. "There are a lot of things in this life that I can put up with…but falling for a junkie? I don't think I could deal with that."

Lurch lit a cigarette. Exhaling he said, "So instead of spending Friday night with a gorgeous girl, you're sitting here in your bedroom with me, drinking wine!"

I just looked at him for a moment, then with a sort of brotherly love, I said, "Oh, I don't know. It's not all that bad, man. You know you and I have been through quite a bit together?"

He just sat, grinning and nodding his head slowly up and down. I bummed a smoke from him, and the two of us just sat there, smoking, drinking wine, and silently reminiscing. We sat there for a couple of moments, almost awkwardly, smoking and thinking back to parts of our life together.

Breaking the silence, I looked over at him and said, "Boy! You sure knocked the hell out of Son that day!"

Lurch looked over to me, sort of surprised. He chuckled. "Well…he pissed me off…the little pinhead!"

Somehow, that sent me into a fit of laughter. When I finally caught my breath, I said, "Pinhead? Do you say pinhead?"

"Yep," he assured me. "That's what I said!"

We were obviously both feeling the effects of the beer and wine by now. Then he started to laugh. "And what about you and that stupid sombrero?" We both roared with laughter then!

"Say, Buddy!" he gasped. "Do you remember that night you were with that one girl, and we were dropping her off at her house? You got out and were kissing her good night, and I accidentally popped the clutch and ran over your bare foot?"

"Yeah," I said. "How could I forget?"

He continued, "Then we stopped at that 7-Eleven, and the guy that works there asked who you thought you were, bleeding all over his floor. You looked up at him really serious and said, 'Just call me Bloody.'"

Lurch was laughing really hard now, but it took me a moment to get back into the spirit of things.

"Yeah," I said. "But I don't think popping the clutch was an accident though. I always figured that you did it on purpose—for whatever reason." A few seconds passed, then I looked back at him. "Hey, what about the night we dropped that dude headfirst into the outhouse on God's Island?"

Lurch held out his hand, and we shook on that one.

Just about that time, we were interrupted by a strange yet familiar voice. "Hey!" it said. "What are you guys doing in here?"

It was George! "Hey, Smolsey," I said, jumping up and throwing my arms around him. Lurch just held out his hand for a handshake right from his seated position, but I could see that he was as happy to see George as I was.

"Hey, man," I said. "Do you want a beer?"

"Definitely!" he answered. "Look, I brought a couple of six-packs with me…they're out in the car."

"I'll go get them," Lurch offered. "I'm ready for another one anyway." He scrambled up a little awkwardly. He had put away a few already, you remember. He went on out toward the car.

George turned and looked over at me. "So what's been happening, Buddy?" More or less making conversation, I guess. "How's your love life?"

I wrinkled my face up a little and told him, "I've decided to put my love life on hold for a while."

I went on to tell him what had happened between Melissa and me, and by the time I was through, here came Lurch with one of the six-packs, telling George he put the other one in the fridge.

"Whoa!" I said. "Tall boys?" (Sixteen-ounce cans.) "Well, boys," I said. "I think from here on out, it's nothing but abuse."

George reached over and grabbed one of the cans then, popping the top, asked, "So what were you guys talking about when I came in? Something about a guy in an outhouse?"

Lurch and I once again shook hands. "Go on," he insisted with a little wave of his hand. "Tell him about it, Buddy."

"Okay... I suppose." I grabbed myself another beer and settled in to tell the tale. "I don't know if you've ever heard of God's Island or not...but to get there, you have to take the causeway out toward Fort De Soto Park. There's a 7-Eleven on the right side of the road that you turn in at. Then beside the store is a dirt trail that winds down to the water. You can only get to the island, of course, by boat.

"We had an old wooden johnboat out there. I don't know whom it belonged to, but anyway, that's the one we used. It had a couple of small holes in it, so when we poled across to the island, someone had to be there with a bucket to bail the water out. It was pretty spooky going out there at night, and the really cool thing was the water was loaded with phosphorus, so when the poles rippled through the water, it lit up in bright fluorescent green."

George then chimed in. "How far away was the island?"

"I don't know," I said. "It probably took us around ten minutes to get out there. The reason we called it God's Island was because there was a trail in the back of the house that if you followed it, you came up on a big cross, probably twenty feet tall. Out by where we pulled the boat in, not too far away was the outhouse. Anyway, a bunch of us were out there one Saturday night partying pretty heavy. There was this guy out there... I really don't remember who he was or who brought him."

I turned to Lurch. "Did you ever know who he was?"

He just shook his head no.

"At any rate," I said, "this dude went down to use the outhouse. He took the official outhouse flashlight with him. A couple of minutes later, he came in and barged right into the conversation. 'Guys! Guys!' he said. 'Somebody's got to help me. I dropped my wallet in the john!' After everyone finally quit laughing, I and Lurch decided we would go to see if we could help him.

"So the three of us headed down the path toward the outhouse. When we got to the outhouse, this dude started shining the light down into that dark hole. It was a good thing he wasn't holding a match—he would have blown us all to kingdom come. Then Lurch asks him, snickering, 'What color is it?' Lurch and I were chuckling, but this guy didn't see the humor in that question. Then the guy says seriously, 'I think if you guys can lower me down, I'll be able to grab it!'

"We just looked at each other as if to say, 'You've got to be kidding?' Then the dude says, 'Come on, guys, you have to help me!' Then he kneels down on the floor in front of the seat, and we each grabbed one of his ankles. We managed to raise him up then slowly lower him down into the hole. He kept telling us, 'Easy guys...easy...easy.'

"Everything seemed to be going pretty good until I looked over at Lurch. That was a big mistake. He had this really evil grin on his face, and I knew right away what he was thinking. I shook my head and whispered, *No man, no!* while all the time he was looking at me, nodding his head up and down and whispering, *Yes, yes.* I just kept shaking my head no, but he started to mouth the words *one...two... three!*

"He let go first, and then I let go because there was no way I could hold this guy by myself. Then we looked over at each other, not really believing what we had just done. It was a moment frozen in time. Quickly we were brought back to reality by this guy in the hole, thrashing around, screaming at us, calling us every name in the book plus a few I think he made up. So we decided to run back to the house, telling each other, 'I can't believe we did that,' not even wondering whether or not this guy could get out of there.

"So now we're back in the house, sitting quietly with the occasional chuckle. Then all of a sudden, we heard this bone-chilling scream trailing through the woods followed by a large splash out by where the boat was docked. It was the dude, of course, taking a much-needed bath. Then Lurch looks over at me and says, 'I sure hope he found his wallet!' That was enough to send the two of us off laughing again. Nobody else in the house could figure out what was so funny to the two of us!"

All the time I was telling George the story, he just stared at me with a look of disbelief.

Now the three of us were laughing pretty hard. George looked at me and said, "I have to admit, that's a pretty good story!"

"No, no!" Lurch piped up. "You haven't heard the best part! Tell him, Buddy."

"Yeah, yeah, that's not the end of the story," I continued. "So here sat the two of us, not really wanting to tell anybody else what we just did when in walks this dude, completely naked from his dip in the gulf. Well…the girls were enjoying it anyway! As we all sat there with our mouths gaped open, Lurch and I were wondering what our next move would be. How much trouble were we going to be in with this guy?

"So he walks over and stands right in front of us—buck naked, mind you. He looks down at us, takes a big deep breath then exhales and says, 'Man, I could really use a beer!' At that point, we looked at each other and pretty much decided maybe this guy was okay—either that or a glutton for punishment."

When the laughter had died down, George said, "I can't believe you guys actually did that."

"Yeah," Lurch said. "I can't believe it either."

I piped up. "What are you talking about? It was your idea!"

Now the mood was sort of changing in that room. Lurch seemed to be deep in thought, and George sat back and nursed his beer while thinking about the story I had just told him. I was trying to figure out what Lurch was thinking about. It was getting pretty quiet, and somehow I didn't like that. Finally, I couldn't take it any longer. "Hey, man," I said to Lurch. "What's on your mind?"

He looked back at me, a little surprised. "What?"

Again I said, "What are you thinking about?"

He paused for a few seconds, then he looked at me with a real sincere look on his face, sort of like the one he wore just before he had told me about Dawn cheating on me. "Well," he said, combing his hair with his fingers. "I guess…" Then he paused again. "I was going to tell you sooner or later. I think I'm going to move out. I just didn't want to leave you here with…you know…everybody. I didn't want you to get mad at me."

Just then, he noticed a smile coming across my face.

"What are you smiling at?" he asked.

I started to belly laugh. "I'm smiling because I'm moving out too—and I didn't know how to tell you!"

"Wait a minute," chimed George. "You're both moving out? So where are you going?"

"My mom is moving out with my sister, so I'm taking over the house. Where are you going?" I asked.

He said he was moving in with a friend of ours named Rick. He, again, was one of our childhood friends. He and Lurch had grown up together on the same street, so they were really close friends.

So here sat the three of us, the originals. It seemed sort of fitting because that was the way it all had started. George had left first, and now Lurch and I were also leaving. I was just as shocked when I thought about his moving out as he probably was about mine. I think that we both knew, though, that it was probably time to move on. With all the drugs that were moving through that house, it would surely only be a matter of time before the cops came down on us, and I don't know if I mentioned this before—but our landlord was a cop!

After all, it wasn't like we'd never see each other again. I was thankful that I had been there and I had lived through it. Looking back, I was glad the three of us had decided to rent this place. Lord, the memories I have of living in that little commune. I'll never forget them, and I could probably fill a whole book with just memories from that house. Yes, there are some things mixed in among them that I'd just as soon forget—but I guess that's just life.

One of the main reasons that I was happy to leave this place behind me was that I figured that by getting out of this atmosphere, I could maybe straighten myself up. Little did I know at that time that my life would still be on the downward trend for a while and I certainly hadn't hit rock bottom yet!

CHAPTER 13

Things were moving along pretty quickly now. The next morning, Lurch was packed and gone before I even could say, "See you later." Either he was a man on a mission, or he didn't feel like telling everybody goodbye. As for me, it took a couple of weeks to get in touch with my cousin and discuss arrangements. Mom, in the meantime, was really looking forward to her move and was busy getting her things together. The old neighborhood was getting kind of rough, and I think she was a little bit scared about that.

After I woke up that Saturday morning, it didn't take me long to remember what I had promised to do the night before—to take back the sombrero I had borrowed from Saul. After all, I was way past due in returning it, and I just hoped that he wasn't mad at me. Regardless, I had to return it, so that's what I did. I grabbed the hat and my keys and headed for his house.

That is, I headed for Saul's by way of the 7-Eleven to grab a cup of coffee first. You know—you need to have your priorities straight. Then I headed for Saul's, and after about ten minutes of driving, I pulled into the driveway. I could see that he and probably his parents were both at home this morning. Saul and his parents were Cuban. He had told me once that his mother actually went to school with Fidel Castro. I suppose somebody had to keep Fidel company.

I knocked on the door, and when Saul's mother answered, she told me he was in his room and that I should go on in. As I walked toward his room, though, I couldn't shake the feeling that something wasn't quite right. I had never seen his mom in such a solemn mood. Maybe she was just mad at him for some reason. The door to his room was halfway open, so I just walked on in with his hat in my hand. "Well," I said. "Better late than never."

He was sitting on the edge of his bed, blankly staring out the window. I, of course, expected him to stand up and greet me. He didn't even acknowledge my presence, and I wondered if he had heard me? Seeing him like that and remembering the mood his mother was in, I figured something was definitely wrong. So I called to him again, a little louder this time. He finally heard me and turned around.

Seeing me, he said, "Oh…hey, man." Instead of getting up and greeting me, he just turned back toward the window. He then spoke, "So what are you doing?"

When he first turned toward me, I could see that his eyes were red as if he had been crying. This really freaked me out!

"Hey, man," I said. "I brought back your sombrero. Sorry to have it so long."

"Oh yeah," he said. "Just hang it on the wall." It was obvious to me that he was not in the mood to talk, but it really seemed that he needed to.

"Okay," I said to him, and I hung the hat back up on his rack. Then I looked across to my friend. He was still looking out the window. "Hey, man," I said after a pause. "Is everything okay? I mean… well, you're not…acting right …you know."

He finally turned around then so I could see him. I saw that his eyes were starting to tear up again. Then he blurted out those awful words: "Bob's dead, man!"

His words hit me like a sledgehammer. I stared over at him, speechless, not believing what he had said—certainly not wanting to believe it.

"You mean… Bobby? Our Bobby? How can that be? I thought he just went to boot camp?"

The Vietnam War was raging at that time, and a lot of boys were dying over there. They weren't dying in boot camp though. I had gone to school with Bobby. He and Saul had met somewhere else, and they had become best friends. The more I partied with Saul, the closer I had gotten to Bobby. I couldn't believe it—one of my friends died? This wasn't supposed to happen—at least not in boot camp.

After I finally got over the shock of it, I asked him how it happened. I had a hard time swallowing the answer I got back.

He asked me if I remembered how much Bobby loved his motorcycle.

"Yeah," I said.

Then he asked me if I had known that the two of them had dreamed of the day when they would both have choppers and ride together. I hadn't known that.

Saul told me that Bobby had gotten a weekend pass, and he was going to check out a Harley that was for sale. He had seen the ad in the local newspaper. He had called Saul to tell him about it. He asked him that if he bought it, could he have it shipped back to Saul's house. Saul had agreed wholeheartedly. So he went over to the guy's house who was selling the bike and wanted to take it for a test ride. The guy agreed, and Bobby took off down the road on his test ride. He never made it back. A car pulled out in front of him, and he hit it going full speed. The crash killed him.

I could see how Saul was feeling; however, I wasn't really sure how I felt. I did know that I wasn't feeling really good. I didn't know what to do, so I just sat down there on the bed next to Saul.

All I could say was, "Damn, man, that's a bummer!"

Saul replied, still looking out the window, "Tell me about it!"

We just sat there in the room for about another ten minutes, not saying anything really, just staring out the window together. I felt that nothing I could say to him would help, so I just kept him company. Finally, I just couldn't take it anymore. I told him I had to be going.

"Okay, man, see you around," he said.

I had almost gotten to the door when he called to me. "So," he said. "I guess it's true what they say about motorcycles."

I nodded back at him. "Yeah… I guess so, man." Then I walked out.

As I walked out and got into my car, I couldn't help but remember a funeral I had been to where another guy that I had known had been killed on a motorcycle. Bobby had been the first one, however, that I had known well. I was starting to realize that death was a really big part of life. Now Bobby was dead. I knew it was an accident, but I also knew that I wouldn't soon understand why those things have to happen.

I headed on over to where my cousin had been staying. He was renting a room from a nice old lady that needed a little extra money. After I got over there, we sat down in the kitchen and had a cup of coffee while we talked. We decided that we would go ahead and take over mom's house. I told him a friend of mine named Dave was looking for a place to stay, and he didn't know why he shouldn't go in with us too, seeing as how it was a three-bedroom house. One thing was pretty definite, though, there was no way we were going to have a whole house full of people like we ended up with at my old place. He had been over there a couple of times to visit me, and that lifestyle just was not his cup of tea. He would say, "It's a nice place to party, but I wouldn't want to live there." He called it the "Hippie Hotel." That was fine with me, of course. I figured that living with Bob and Dave would be, well, a more normal sort of existence. I was ready for a little of that about then. If I ever got lonesome, there was nothing to keep me from just heading down to the Rocks for a while.

After my little talk with Bob, I headed home and made my official announcement to everyone there that I'd be moving out in a week. Real quick, like Vicky and Jimmy pounced on the chance for my room. I guess they were getting tired of their accommodations in the attic.

Moving day was here. Notice I didn't say "finally here" or "here at last" because I didn't really have any emotional feelings about it one way or another. I was just going back home as I had done several times before in my life. The only difference was that this time, Mom and Dad wouldn't be there. Mom would be about half an hour down the road. Dad, on the other hand, was gone for good. I wouldn't have to worry about him any longer. Even though I was enjoying my independence, I have to admit that there were times when I sorely missed that man. I was and am glad that when I remembered him, the times that I always thought of were the good times that we had together like the time we spent in the backyard, playing catch; going to see the Harlem Globetrotters together, just him and me; the time that he took me deep-sea fishing; and yes, even the times at the hospital when he was nearing the end. It might sound strange to you that I would include those times at the hospital among the good times, but it seemed somehow that when he and I were alone in the hospital room together, we could talk to one another like we had never talked before. Some sort of barrier that existed between us at any other time just seemed to sort of evaporate away, and we could talk together on a man-to-man basis.

One of those times when they rushed my dad to the hospital, they tried to give him a medical treatment of some sort, but dad wasn't thinking too straight and tried to fight them off. He was a stubborn old guy, and I'm sure he was just tired of being in hospitals and having people poking at him. He had always been a very powerful man, and I guess he hadn't lost much of that strength. The upshot of it was they finally ended up having to put a straitjacket on him to control him.

The next day the crisis passed, and Dad was in his right mind again. I went to visit him in the hospital the next day. Now if that had been me, I probably wouldn't have said a thing to my son about the incident—but there he was, telling me all about the experience. Then as he was talking, he reached over and pulled that straitjacket out of the drawer!

"Here it is." His voice seemed almost proud as he held it in front of him. "They left it here for me. Here! You try it on!"

I wasn't so sure that was a good idea. I was thinking that if he had a pair of scissors in that drawer, he'd never be able to pass up the opportunity to cut my hair, but I could see that he wanted me to put it on; so I wrapped myself up in it, and I'll never forget his laughing—he was really enjoying himself—as I turned and twisted and tried to get out of the bind I was in. Even though the hysterics were at my expense, in a manner of speaking, at least, it really didn't bother me. Now that I think of it, that was the only time I can remember that the two of us really ever joked and laughed together. I guess that's why that memory will always be precious to me. It certainly was a shame that I had to wait until he was on his deathbed that we decided to just accept one another for who we were.

Now moving day had arrived. It was Saturday morning, around ten thirty. I had to get up early that day to pack my stuff and to meet my cousin Bob at the old homestead by noon. One good thing, there was no need to call Mayflower or Allied Van lines. I stuffed my things into the trunk and backseat of the car, and I was ready to go. Like I said before, there were no sentimental feelings or heartfelt regrets. It was just as if the party was finally ending, and it was time to go home—except, of course, that this party had lasted for six months! People had come and gone. Chris, Danny, George, Lurch, and I were gone now. After Joe and Phil heard the news of us leaving, they started talking about going back to New York. I don't know if they ever did. I never managed to get back to the house after that day. Jack was working steadily and had been since he and Gail moved in with us. Gail was really wanting for them to find their own place. They had been saving their money, so they were looking for something they could afford. Jimmy and Vicky? Well, they were comfortable just riding things out. They were anxious to move into their bedroom and out of the attic, however.

I had the car packed up and was ready to go. I had sold my drums to Roach, the guy I had originally bought them from, so I had plenty of room for all my stuff. I took one last look around—mainly, I guess, because it just seemed to be the thing to do. Lord knows I realized that there was nothing holding me here any longer. I decided it was time, so I headed out the door for the last time. I bopped down the steps then turned for one last admiring look at that giant yellow Mr. Sun that Lurch had painted on the chimney. As I stood there looking up at it one last time, I heard a familiar sound—the squeak of a screen door at the nursing home behind me.

That squeak had become very familiar to me the past few months. I had heard it the night I had intercepted Joe and Phil and their lone Big Mac before they could get into the house, the night that Melissa and I had sat out on the front stoop and awkwardly found our way into each other's hearts. As a matter of fact, I think I heard that squeak, well, practically every day I had lived there. I turned to look across the road to the nursing home, for this would, after all, probably be my last glimpse of it. There he stood—the old man—the one who had excitedly yelled "fight" the day that Lurch lit into Son, the one who had laughed so hard that morning when George and I had gone out to retrieve the green chair from the bus stop. I just stood there for a moment and stared over at him, and he, in turn, stared back at me. Did he somehow sense that things were changing? Was he watching me load my car and knew I was leaving? Then for some reason, one of those heartfelt emotions sort of just snuck up on me by surprise. Maybe I was leaving something behind, after all, but what? He was nothing to me—or was he? Maybe in my subconscious, that old man represented the one thing I was most afraid of—reality! Then once again, I found myself looking at me and my friends from his point of view. Who knew, maybe there was something about the antics of this crazy house across the street that made him yearn to be young once more, or maybe it was a matter of memory—his memories of things in his day, the sorts of things that we were doing in ours. As for us, our memories were still in the making. One of mine that I would take fondly with me through the years would be that shaky old man standing on the porch across the street.

I figured it would be a really awkward thing for me to go over there. I had never done that—it was probably a little late for that. So I decided to do the next best thing; something I hadn't done before, come to think of it. I raised my hand up by my face and gave a couple of short waves. He just stood there and looked at me for a moment. I couldn't see him well enough to catch any facial expression; we were too far away from each other for that. I would have loved to have known what he was thinking at that moment. Then after a few more seconds, he raised his hand and waved back at me.

I nodded to him then and muttered under my breath, "See you, old man. Take care of yourself!" Then I walked over to the car, got in, and drove away. I didn't know him and he didn't know me. One thing was for sure—if he was my guardian angel, he sure didn't stick around very long!

Whenever I had gone home before, it had usually been because I had lost a job or a place to stay. Mom always told me no matter what happened, I could always come home! This time, the feeling wasn't quite so warm because it wasn't home anymore, of course; it was just a house. Things got even weirder when I found out that Bob had claimed my old room and I ended up sleeping in Mom and Dad's room and their bed!

That first night was like the twilight zone revisited. I had trouble sleeping that night, even reinforced as I was by several drinks— several drinks? I guess that's the way to put it. Bob and I had started drinking just after noon that day, then about four o'clock, we went out for a pizza and more beers. So you can understand that by seven o'clock or so, we were getting pretty toasted. I ended up going to bed early and lay awake far into the night sleeping in my parents' bed! Well, I guess it was only natural that I should think about them most of the night.

Right before I finally did drift off, however, I thought, *I wonder what the inmates are doing right about now?* I figured Joe and Phil were just about getting home with the snacks. You wouldn't believe the sudden yen I got for a Big Mac! But it passed eventually, and I slid off to dreamland.

As time went by, living with Bob and Dave (yeah Dave finally made it), I found that I was partying less but drinking more. Do you know what I mean? Well, you see I had gotten a job with Bob doing carpenter work, building forms on a high-rise building. We were together practically all the time. We rode together back and forth to work, naturally, and every day we would either grab a six-pack and a block of cheddar cheese for the ride home or else stop at a bar. Either way, it meant I was handling a lot of brew. The upshot of all of this was that my drinking was gradually turning from a weekend thing to a full-time affair. So what this meant was that now, I was catching a buzz all week long—getting hammered on the weekends.

So where did we go? Sometimes Bob went to the Rocks with me, but usually, we ended up at a bar called Dickie Doo's, Bob's favorite hangout. Yes, sir, I was now hanging out with drunks of a much higher caliber! I had fun, though, getting to know some of the people there. I remember there was this one old shell-shocked ex-marine, whose name was also Bob. When things started getting a little dull, someone would always scream out, "Ten-hut!" It was just like Pavlov's dog when he rang the bell. Bob the old marine would jump up, salute, and march around the bar high stepping and calling out cadence as loud as he could. It was funny the first couple of times, but after that, Dick, the owner, would put a stop to it. I mean, after all, this man serving in the Marines and fighting for his country was not something to be made fun of.

Also at the bar was still another guy named Bob. There were sure a lot of Bobs that went there. This one, however, had a daughter named Melissa. Yeah, you remember her. She never came around the place—at least whenever I was there. Every time I saw him, I was always reminded of her. I wondered if he knew about her addiction? I was never tempted to bring it up; however, sometimes I would wonder how it might have turned out for me and Melissa. And after a while, the memory just faded.

So for a while, one day just sort of slid into the next one. Work was steady, and I was really beginning to pick up on this carpentry stuff. The problem was my drinking was going full speed by this time. Now, two or three days a week, the guys from work would head down to this little beach bar for lunch. I would get a burger or a hotdog off the rotisserie and drink a couple of beers to wash down the food. So now I was drinking for lunch and dinner—but at least I just drank coffee for breakfast?

As things turned out, Bob wasn't going to be with Dave and me for long. He met a woman around his own age named Pam, who worked at the local dairy. The good thing about this was that she always had plenty of cottage cheese in the refrigerator. As it happened, Bob and I were on this protein kick. We both loved cottage cheese. Bob and I would eat anything over cottage cheese—gravy, tomato soup, chicken noodle soup, vegetable beef soup—anything that was available. As it turned out, our source of dairy products dried up about it as soon as it started. Pam had been divorced and had a five-year-old son, and while I don't know positively that this had anything to do with things, but something did. She and Bob broke up. I was sorry to see that happen and not just because of the cottage cheese either—she was good people!

Bob must have been at that stage of life where he was looking to settle down because it wasn't long before he had met another woman, this one named Paula. They hit it off pretty good—so good, in fact, that after a couple of months of going with her, Bob announced that he was going to get married. The funny thing was Paula had also been divorced, and she had two sons. Go figure that one out?

But the good part of it was that Bob and I would still be working together, and he would still be picking me up for work. That meant, of course, that he could still drag me out of bed if I happened to have been up a little late partying the night before. Another thing that was working out so far, as this particular situation was concerned, was Luann's situation. Remember that day down at the Rocks when I had seen her and found out that she would be losing her house? Now that Bob had moved out, that left Dave and I with an extra bedroom—not to mention a third of the rent not being covered. So I decided I would see if she wanted the extra bedroom because I was such a good friend? After all, the rent on the house was only $60 a month, and that would break down to her share being only $10 a week for rent and utilities. Surely she could handle that!

It's not like I was planning to fall in love again, mind you. I was a changed man determined not to fall for anyone ever again. Besides, ever since I had moved in with my cousin, I was sort of operating under a different set of rules. Bob had given me postgraduate instruction in the art of the one-night stand—which, of course, made his long-term relationships with Pam and Paula so puzzling when they had occurred. I was determined that falling in love from now on would be limited to one night at a time. I had long since given up on the "match made in heaven" idea. I was a free agent now, and I sort of planned on keeping it that way.

It troubled me in a way because I had lost the warm feeling that I got inside when I met a girl for the first time. Now instead of being genuine and sincere, the only thing I was concerned about was keeping score. It had all just become a game to me. I would literally tell the girls anything they wanted to hear just to win them over. I had told the same old lies over and over again—so much that I had started to believe them myself. What it really came down to was that

I had gotten to the point in my life where I had no direction what-soever. As long as I had a roof over my head and enough money to make the scene, I was happy. And of those two priorities, the latter certainly outweighed the former. I let the house go and didn't even cut the grass anymore. Oh yeah, I was happy—or so I thought. The problem was that the more I drank, the more it was the drinking that mattered. Give Dawn credit; at least she knew that she had to get her you know together. I didn't even realize what my life was becoming.

Why mention Dawn again, you ask? Oh, my adventures with her were far from over. All the time I was busy becoming a drunk, she was busy getting her life together—sort of? Like a line from an old Bob Dylan song, the truth—she was working in a topless joint, and I stopped in for a beer.

CHAPTER 14

Actually, as it happened, it was Lurch and I that stopped in for a beer. It was a Friday evening, and I stopped in at the Rocks for old times' sake and a drink. Looking around, whom should I see but Lurch, sitting all alone with his back sort of turned to the action. At first, I thought maybe something was bothering him, but it turned out that he was just fine. Then I thought that maybe he was praying, but when I asked him about that, he was embarrassed by my question.

"Me? Pray?" he said disdainfully. "No, I wasn't praying! I don't even think I know how to pray?"

What he was doing, it seemed, was something he had never done before in his life. He was in the midst of—as he put it—just getting drunk.

"Well," I said. "If that's what you're doing, you've come to the right place." But what I really wanted to say was, "It's a damn sight better than needles!" Then again, who was I to judge?

Now when I ordered a beer, I asked for a shot of Southern comfort to go with it. I had gotten to the point where just beer wasn't enough. As we were sitting there, getting reacquainted, I glanced around the place and could see why I had picked him out so randomly. The usual crowd didn't seem to be on duty that night.

"Hey, where is everybody tonight?" I asked.

Lurch took another swig of beer. "Probably down at the topless bar," he opined. "That's where a lot of people have been going lately…hell, they probably won't even have a band here tonight. Crowds are too small these days…"

"Whoa, whoa, whoa!" I said. "Topless bar? What topless bar? I had been over on the mainland for so long going to Dickie Doo's I hadn't even heard of this."

A sort of a conniving look came over his face, one that didn't really register on me until later. Now I realize that what he was thinking was if I hadn't heard about this bar, I certainly wouldn't know that Dawn was working there. That being the case, why not take me over there?

At the time, though, I just sat there naively as Lurch replied, "Oh, yeah, man, the old beach pub. Somebody bought it and turned it into a topless bar…say, do you know what we ought to do? We ought to go over there right now and check it out. I haven't been there either," he said, and of course, he was lying through his teeth all the time—but I didn't know that.

"Nah," I replied. "I'm not interested, and besides, I hear those places are usually pretty expensive."

Lurch was back on me again. "Come on, man, let's go! Tell you what, I'll spring for the first round."

Now I should have known that something was up because he and I had been good friends for a long time, but he never offered to buy drinks. I suppose it was worth a few dollars to him to see the look on my face.

"All right," I conceded. "Let's go!"

He looked down at the empty shot glass on the table. "Hey, man, that doesn't include shots. You have to buy them."

* * * * *

We were heading toward the door now.

"When did you start drinking shots with your beer anyway?" Lurch inquired.

"Oh, I've been hanging out at this bar with my cousin lately. A lot of the people over there have shots with their beer. I decided to try it one night, and I liked it. I just do it once in a while because I can't afford it all the time."

He made a little grunt in the back of his throat. Shaking his head, he said, "Don't you know stuff'll kill you?"

I grinned over to him with raised eyebrows. "Right! Whatever you say!"

By this time, we were near to the topless bar. Even on the sidewalk outside, I could hear the blare of the music inside. As we entered the place it was like a wave engulfing us. It was so loud that I soon made up my mind that if there was to be any communication here, it would have to be by screaming—just right, as far as I was concerned, at that point in my life.

After a quick look around, I could see what he meant by a lot of the crowd from the Rocks coming down here now. Man, there were a lot of people we knew here—even Jimmy and Vicky were there. I wasn't surprised, though, when I didn't see Lora.

Meanwhile, Lurch was screaming in my ear, "I think I see a table!"

Lurch's plan was working beautifully, of course. We hadn't seen Dawn yet, and he had me, well, right where he wanted. As we sat and waited for a waitress, I just let my eyes drift around the bar. It seemed the more I did this, I would catch the eye of someone I knew. I'd smile and give a little wave of my hand. This place was definitely busy, but the service was really slow.

I leaned over to scream in Lurch's ear, "Where is the waitress?" while grabbing my throat and sticking out my tongue as if I was dying of thirst.

Just then a big smile covered his face, and I naturally thought that I had been the cause of that smile until I saw him pointing to someone behind me. As he did so, he mouthed the words, "the waitress, the waitress!" I had been so successful in amusing him with my little "dying of thirst" routine that I thought maybe I could score some points with the waitress too! With my tongue still hanging out and my hands still clutching my throat, I turned to face the waitress—and lo and behold, it was Dawn! Guess what? She wasn't smiling either, and she was clad in nothing but a G-string!

The shock of seeing her standing there was so great that I just automatically stood up, nearly choking for real. Meanwhile, of course, Lurch was laughing so hard at me and my reaction that he was turning red in the face. Still standing and in shock, I turned to him; and pointing behind myself, I mouthed the words "That's Dawn! That's Dawn!" just as if he didn't recognize her. All he could do was nod in agreement.

Dawn, meanwhile, stood there with her hands on her hips, not at all happy with this turn of events. She screamed in my ear, "What do you want, Buddy?" And meanwhile, I was looking back and forth from her to Lurch, trying to get my brain into gear. What I really wanted to say was "I want…to not be here!"

Finally, I calmed down enough to stammer, "Uh…two Buds, I guess," but I didn't have things together enough, I guess, to realize that I had to pump up the volume on my order a little. So she pulled her hair back behind her ear and leaned in toward me. Taking my cue from this, I screamed in her ear this time: "Two Buds, please! She nodded and went off in the direction of the bar.

I don't know why, but for some reason I found myself feeling sorry for her. This was really sort of a tacky setup that Lurch had pulled, and I was sure that she must have been much more embarrassed even than I had been. In addition, I found myself wondering, *Why did she have to work in a place like this anyway? Couldn't she find a job somewhere else?*

Along about then, my thoughts were interrupted by a spotlight hitting the stage immediately in front of me. It was time for one of the girls to come out and dance. As you may have guessed, it was her turn. The evening couldn't have turned out better for Lurch, of course; he was having a ball at my expense. And just think he got it all for the price of a couple of beers which I found out later cost him five dollars a glass! I could get a twelve-ounce bottle at the Rocks for just one dollar.

I was embarrassed for her—I really was! I'm sure that it was tough on her too, my being there, I guess. Actually, I was surprised at how embarrassed I was. Maybe I still cared a little for her. I don't know—anyway, I just couldn't bring myself to watch. As a matter of fact, as inconspicuously as I could, I scooted my chair around a bit so that my back was turned toward her. I thought that it would help a bit, but it really didn't.

I don't know how long she danced that night; it couldn't have been more than two or three minutes, I guess. It seemed to take hours. Finally, it was over, and the music stopped, and the spotlight went off. I gave a sigh of relief, but then I saw that she was coming down the steps that were on the side of the stage and heading directly toward me.

She peered into my eyes and said in a voice dripping with venom, "Well, stud, what's the matter...you too embarrassed to watch?"

Now there was a lot of noise in that place, but even so, she said that to me just after the music had stopped and she had come down off the stage. I'm sure that at least half of the people who were there heard what she had said to me. I knew that I didn't want to make a scene here in front of all these people, so I decided that things would be best if I just left as quickly as possible. So I stood up, looked over at Lurch, and told him I was going back to the Rocks! I thought that would let us all calm down as gracefully as possible. I suppose she was still a little upset, as I guess she had a right to be.

Then she pushed me—figuratively and literally—and said in the same tone of voice. "Well, are you? Are you embarrassed?"

I took a deep breath and somehow managed to stay calm. "No, I'm not embarrassed!" I said. "Look at you! You're the one who should be embarrassed, not me." Then I gulped down the remainder of my beer and left as quickly as I could.

I went outside and headed toward the Rocks, as I had said I would. Lurch didn't follow me. I guess he figured that I was mad at him now, but I really wasn't. After all, I knew that he hadn't meant any harm in taking me down there. What I was feeling was I was upset with myself for letting her get to me again. Damn! That was before the movie *Jaws* came out, but that was the feeling that I had— "just when I thought it was safe."

After a couple of minutes' walk, I entered the bar. As I looked around, I noticed there still weren't many people there and there was no one that I knew. At that point, I just decided to go on home and call it a night. I had gotten up early that morning for work, so I was pretty tired. I would stop on the way home and get a bite to eat somewhere and then head home.

When I got home, no one was there either, and it was really quiet and restful. I went to the fridge and popped a beer and then just sat down and reflected on what had happened earlier that evening. I could never have imagined that Dawn would end up working in a place like that. Was she that desperate? What had happened to the waitress job that she seemed so happy about? Again, I felt myself feeling sorry for her. Maybe, just maybe, way down deep inside, I still had feelings for her. One thing was for sure—I was tired of thinking about it. I decided to head off to bed. Besides, tomorrow is another day! Saturday! I was going to get to sleep in!

CHAPTER 15

Saturday morning came, and I woke up at about nine o'clock to sunshine pouring into my bedroom window. Due to the fact that I hadn't consumed that much alcohol the night before, I felt great. I got up and headed toward the kitchen to make a cup of coffee—instant coffee, that is. Mr. Coffee hadn't been invented yet, so I fixed it in my usual manner—heat up some water on the stove, mix in the instant, then add milk and sugar. I went back into the living room to sit and enjoy my coffee, still having the house to myself. It was a really nice day out today.

I decided I would get energetic today. I would clean the house, clean the kitchen, and yes, I decided to get out the old lawnmower and cut the grass. I would spend the day doing positive things—doing things that needed to be done that I had been neglecting. After all that was done, I actually gathered up some dirty clothes and went to the laundromat. I was feeling really good about myself, almost like a responsible adult! I got back from the laundromat, put my clothes away, took a bath, and then decided to sit down and have a beer. As the saying went, I was all dressed up and had no place to go.

Not quite the case as I did have a place to go—back down to the Rocks, of course. Maybe tonight would be a better night than last night was. So off I went, headed to the bar. When I got close, I noticed there were a lot more cars parked there tonight than the night before. I parked the car, got out, and went in. As I walked through the place looking from side to side for some familiar faces, I couldn't believe my eyes. It was my old buddy Moe—he was shooting pool.

He and I had met in high school and had become best friends. In our junior year, we had gym class together. We had to put our initials on our gym clothes. His initials were GI. Since there was already a G. I. Joe, we decided we would call him G. I. Moe. Anyway, the name caught on pretty quickly; and after a while, we dropped the GI and it just became Moe. He ended up really liking that nickname and didn't want to be called anything else after that. After high school, I was the only one that knew his real name, and he was the only one that knew my real name. So I guess it just became our little secret. After high school, Moe joined the Navy. It had been a while since I had seen him. Man, was I glad to see him.

He was on a ten-day leave before he had to go back, and he was ready to party. That was okay with me; I was ready too after being reunited with my good friend. We both sucked down a couple of beers apiece and then went on to shots of tequila with salt and lemon. We had partnered up on the pool table and were playing for a dollar a game. That was enough to buy another beer, so as long as we kept winning, our beer was free.

Then we heard a familiar voice talking behind us. I turned around to see another old friend nicknamed Double O. No, not 007, just Double O. I've no idea where he got that one, He was the father of some boys that I grew up with. Of course, we had all gotten to know each other quite well over the years. At one point in my father's life, the two of them had bent an elbow together at a place called the M&M Rendezvous. M&M Rendezvous, Dickie Doo's? I guess if you owned a bar back then, you had to give it a name? What would be wrong with a name like Joe's Place or something?

Anyway, the three of us continued to talk while Moe and I continued shooting pool.

Double O piped up, "Hey, you guys have got to see my new boat." Then he continued, "Yeah, it's an old coast guard boat, a twenty-eight-footer complete with a galley and a couple of bunks down below. I've got it all cleaned up and running pretty well. You guys want to go for a boat ride?"

Now Moe and I were getting pretty well oiled by this time with all the beer and tequila shots. We weren't doing really good at the pool table anymore, so we decided a boat ride would be great fun.

Double O agreed we would go but then said, "We'll have to take Billy with us." The two of them had been out in the boat most of the day, drinking and fishing. Then he looked around the bar. "Now where did he get off to?" he said.

About that time, the men's room door squeaked open, and out staggered Billy. He looked to be in worse shape than the three of us put together. He proceeded to fall down on a chair, lay his head on the table, and go to sleep.

I looked at Double O and said, "Well, he's not going anywhere."

Double O replied, "We can't go anywhere without him. If we go to the boat, he has to come with us. He's my responsibility today."

So the three of us walked back to the table where Billy was sleeping—or unconscious or whatever. Double O started jostling him and shaking him and trying his best to arouse him. "Hey, come on, buddy…wake up, man…we gotta go! It's time to go!"

I put my arm around Double O's shoulder. "Hey, look, man, you're wasting your time on him," I said softly. "He's gone!"

"Well," replied Double O. "We can't go without him!"

Moe and I looked at each other. There was only one thing to do, and we knew it. If that was the only way we were going to get our boat ride, then we might as well see if we could get him up and out to the boat. Without a word, Moe went to one side of him and I went to the other, and we picked him up bodily between us. We had about one hundred yards to drag him out of the bar, across the street, and over to the pier then about halfway down the pier to where the boat was docked. It was no easy task either, let me tell you. Even though Billy wasn't very big, he wasn't helping us at all. Moe and I weren't in that great of shape either, so we basically just dragged him out to the boat. Now it was fast approaching ten o'clock, and we really wanted this boat ride. I don't know why it was that important to us; I guess it was just something to do.

We finally got everybody on board, and we were all glad to be there—well, at least three of us. I doubt Billy even knew where he was at that point. We flopped him down on a lawn chair that was on deck, and Moe and I headed for the bench in the back of the boat. Double O headed up to the helm, started the boat up, and then hollered back for somebody to get him a beer out of the red cooler. Moe and I looked at each other to see who would get that beer. Then Moe finally decided he would take care of it. He opened the lid of the cooler, and there, in partially melted ice, were about twenty bottles of Old Milwaukee. Moe's head snapped back.

"Whoa, baby!" he said. "Damn, Bud, we're on a luxury cruise!" He took a bottle up to the captain then grabbed two more for him and me. There was no need to ask Billy if he wanted one; he was sleeping the sleep of the just and I'm sure wasn't even aware of where he was.

Man, was it dark! All I could see was the light on the front of the boat, and I sure hoped that Double O knew where he was going. As I turned around to look behind us, I could see where we'd been. However, ahead of us was a different story. All I could see was darkness, not even a star in the sky. Moe and I weren't saying much at that point; we just sat there, drinking our beer, as the salt air blew in our faces. We could hear the sound of the water spreading out behind us while we enjoyed our boat ride—finally! We weren't breaking any speed limits, just sort of cruising along nice and easy. Somehow, though, I felt a lot better when Double O decided that we were out far enough and started bringing the boat around to head back to the dock. I could see the neon lights from the bars on shore shining in the distance. It's hard to tell how far out you really are when you're on the water and it's dark and you've been drinking for three or four hours. I was feeling pretty good now, however. We were headed toward shore.

And then, just about the time I was feeling all safe and secure, the engine starting to pop and sputter.

No, I thought as it popped a couple more times and then quit—quit altogether. All was quiet now—I mean really quiet! Sort of eerie too. As I said before, it was really dark out there. I guess the best way to describe the darkness would be if you were wearing sunglasses outside at midnight. So there we were, the four of us, in the middle of that dark harbor. Double O took out his lighter and held it up to the gauges on the dashboard.

After examination, he said calmly, "Well, that's it!" He didn't seem to be concerned about it in the least.

Moe and I just sat there, not believing the predicament we were in.

Finally, I spoke up: "So, what do you mean exactly by 'that's it'?"

"We're out of gas," he answered. "And I didn't bring any extra."

So now Moe piped up, "What do we do now?"

"Well…one of two things," answered Double O. "We either throw the anchor out here so that we don't drift, or we let the boat drift, hoping that we can get a little closer to the shore and then drop the anchor." He paused, smothering a yawn. "Do what you want," he said abruptly. "I'm going to bed." And with that, he crawled down into the bow of the boat where the bunks were and promptly dropped off to sleep.

Moe and I couldn't believe that he would just go off to sleep like that and leave us in this situation. I suppose, looking back on it, that the worst thing that could have happened would have been losing the anchor and drifting all night. The two of us considered all the options and decided to do the responsible thing—we had another beer! Meanwhile, we reconsidered the two options available to us. For the moment, we decided to let the boat drift and see where that would get us. We squinted out through the darkness and decided that we were kind of drifting closer to the point—the only trouble was we didn't seem to be getting any closer to the shore, which, of course, was our objective.

We sat there for a little while longer, nursing our beers and trying to figure out just what the hell we were going to do. The reality of potentially being stranded on this boat all night had a sobering effect on us—well, maybe just a little.

Moe then looked over at me with a serious face and said, "You know, Bud, I think I could make it to shore."

I looked over at him curiously and asked, "What do you mean… swim to shore?"

"Yep," he answered, getting up out of his chair. "I'm gonna swim to shore. I'll be damned if I'm gonna spend all night on this boat!"

It's just astounding all the stupid ideas you can come up with after drinking shots of tequila and beer all night. I guess with booze comes bravery. I wasn't that good of a swimmer even when I was sober. After thinking it over for a couple of minutes, I agreed that's what we would do.

"Sure…what the hell," I said. "I'll give it a try." Notice I didn't say, "What have I got to lose?"

What followed that night would be an experience that I would never forget even though parts of it are still a mystery to me. Moe and I decided that our best plan would be just to swim fully dressed and to put our keys in our wallets and hold our wallets in our teeth to try to keep them dry. I refer back to this sometimes as the "Old Milwaukee plan"!

Moe went in first. "See you on shore," he said just before sticking his wallet in his mouth and swimming off into the darkness."

"Yeah, man!" I shouted after him. "I'm right behind you!"

Okay, now it was my turn. Fully dressed, keys and wallet in my teeth, I couldn't decide if, because I was wearing sandals, that would help me or hinder me. I didn't think about it long before I eased myself into that cold water. I took a deep breath then pushed off the boat, heading toward shore. I focused on one of the street lights on the boulevard and headed straight for it.

It wasn't long before I started to realize that things weren't really going exactly as I'd hoped. For one thing, with my wallet stuck in my mouth like that, I was having difficulty breathing, and my jaw was already beginning to ache from biting down on it so hard to keep it from falling into the water. Then I soon realized that my sandals were more of a hindrance than a help. When I pumped my legs to swim, the water was going in between my foot and the sole of the sandal and holding me back so that it was as if my legs and my arms were almost working against each other. The third thing that was working against me was that now my clothes were soaking wet and seemed to be weighing me down.

All of this threw me into a little bit of a panic. I found myself thinking that if I could just get those sandals off, I could probably make it. With that in mind, I began gouging one foot with the other, desperately trying to rid myself of those sandals—but wouldn't you know it, they were buckled on tightly and just weren't about to come off. I tried reaching down with my hand to force them off physically—but of course, when I did that, I would start to sink under the briny water.

I was really beginning to panic now and tried desperately to determine how far I had come from the boat. Should I try to make it toward the boat now or the shore? I could see the lights on shore vaguely in front of me, and of course, I knew that the boat was somewhere back there behind me. Now, my frightened mind determined that I might be a lot closer to the boat than I was to the shore. Yes, that was what I would do. I should try to get back to the boat if I could see it in this damned darkness!

During my endeavor to rid myself of my sandals, I had swallowed quite a bit of seawater, and I was choking on that. I made another decision and with a twist of my head threw the wallet out of my mouth. My money, driver's license, and my keys all gone into the sea—but how important was any of that at a time like this? I tried to cough up the water I had swallowed and get myself breathing again, but I had been under a couple of other times, and I knew that I was losing control, that, in fact, I was losing the battle. I was in big trouble and on the verge of drowning—drowning in the same water that I had swum and fished in as a kid.

Then something really strange began to happen—the stark panic that has settled upon me began to fade. In its place came a calm like nothing I have ever known before. All of a sudden, I was having visions—or hallucinations, if you prefer to call them that—but the thing of it was they were so crystal clear! Have you ever heard the old cliché about how a drowning man's life flashes before him in an instant? Well, I wasn't seeing my life. I was seeing my death. I saw all my family and friends dressed up in their best clothes and standing around all solemn-like. I didn't know what was happening, but they sure did look sad. My mother was there too, and she was the saddest of all. She was crying, in fact. Then she moved away from the others, and I could see that she was in a funeral home. She went up to a casket, tears streaming from her eyes. She looked down sadly, shaking her head, and there I was in the casket, my eyes closed and my hands crossed over my chest. What was happening to me!

The strangest thing about all of this, as I look back on it, was how calm and peaceful I felt. I was seeing all of this as real as it could be. But I was calm, and yet in a corner of my mind, at least, I knew that I was at that moment drowning. I felt no part of the panic that had filled me earlier. What I felt now was peace for myself and sadness for my mother.

I kept thinking over and over again, *I'm sorry, Mom, I'm really sorry. God, I'm so sorry!*

And then quicker than it takes to tell about it, it all disappeared. I was being hoisted, bodily, out of the water. My mind whirled in confusion. Where was I? Had I died? What was happening? Had I been saved? Then in a second, I realized I was back on the boat—or so it seemed! But how had I gotten here? I fell to my knees. I was exhausted from the struggle I had just experienced. I looked over just in time to see Billy fall back into his chair. Could he have saved me? I called his name a couple of times, but he didn't respond. Could it have been him? I don't see how that could've happened physically, because I was at least a head taller than he was, and I surely outweighed him by at least fifty pounds. Could he have literally pulled me up out of that water and onto the boat?

On shaking legs, I got up and stumbled to the stern of the boat and sank down on the bench there. I tried sorting out in my mind what just happened to me. In the first place, how had I gotten back to the boat? It had been black as pitch, and God only knows how far off a true course I had gotten while trying to get my sandals off. Then shortly after that, I had decided to turn around and go back to the boat. I had gone into that vision—or whatever it was. I hadn't really been consciously in control of my body at all, and yet somehow, I honed right in on the boat. I certainly hadn't had much stamina left in me the last I could remember! Then, too, there was the matter of Billy. Why had he roused himself right at the precise moment that he needed to come to my rescue? And given that, how had he known to look for me? There was no way that I could have made much noise in the condition that I was in. And even after that, how had he managed to haul me in?

Now I recollected how resentful I had been maybe an hour before that Moe and I had to drag him along with us onto the boat. Something very weird or something very wonderful—or both—was going on here! Something well beyond my comprehension had happened to me. I was happy to be alive. Yes, and I was happy for my mom too. You talk about things having a sobering effect on a person—believe me, coming as close to death as I had is definitely the ticket. In spite of all that alcohol that I had been drinking that evening, at that moment, I was sober as a judge.

I was just sort of trying to get all of this straight in my mind when I heard a distant scream from the shore, calling out my name with tones of rising panic. Moe! It was Moe, looking for me, worrying about me. Thank God he had made it to shore. He must have been in an awful panic worrying about me. I scrambled to my feet and leaned across the side of the boat, cupping my mouth with my hands.

"Moe!" I called across the water. "I'm okay..."

I sat back down on the bench and just relaxed. I looked around at the water and then up at the sky. Now things had changed. Now there were stars twinkling in the sky that had not been there before. Then I thought about how my mom had always told me about God's angels. The more I thought about that, the more I realized that it was probably an angel that had pulled me out of that water. Maybe they had used Billy's body to do it, but however it was done, I knew I was extremely thankful.

Now looking out into the water, I noticed a small white light that appeared to be heading straight for us. It turned out to be a man in a small aluminum boat that had been out fishing that night. At this point, of course, getting to shore didn't seem to matter all that much. It's amazing how your priorities can change so quickly.

The boat came within earshot, and I called out for help. The man called back to me.

"Need a tow?"

"Yeah!" I replied. "We're out of gas! Could you haul us to the pier?"

He agreed, so I threw him a line, and off we went. When we docked at the pier, it was almost like my vision a few moments before. There was Moe and a bunch of my friends waiting for me there. They all started clapping!

"Damn, Buddy!" said Moe, coming forward and throwing his arms around me. Both of us were still damp from our late-night swim, but we didn't seem to care very much. "Man! I thought you drowned out there!"

I gave him sort of a grin, nodding. "Yeah," I said. "I thought so too!"

We all had a good laugh then. I didn't let on that I didn't really think it was all that funny. By this time, Double O had gotten up and was helping secure the boat to the pier. Then I sort of separated myself from the group and walked over to the side of the pier.

I looked down at Billy, still contentedly off in dreamland some-where. "Thanks, brother," I said softly. "Thanks for saving my life… if that was you, that is." Then I looked into the sky, feeling very humbled about what I had just been through. "Thank you, God," I whispered, "for watching out for me." The more I thought about it, the more I was convinced—it was an angel that pulled me out of that dark water.

Decades have passed since this happened to me, but one Sunday, while sitting in church, listening to the pastor's sermon, which had to do with miracles, like God parting the Red Sea, I remembered the night I had almost drowned. Then I realized, as only a sober person could have, shouldn't there have been life preservers on that boat?

CHAPTER 16

How long does it take a person to get over a very humbling experience like the one I had just gone through? How about forty-eight hours? It seemed as if from that point onward, even though I had little indication that I might be coming back to reality, things just kept going from bad to worse. And if you've ever been there, you know things can always get worse. Everyone had moved out of my house, so now it was just me paying the bills. The job I was on was winding down, and I, along with about six other carpenters, were laid off. Construction jobs at that time were few and far between, so I did what everyone else seemed to be doing. I collected unemployment, and I partied. It's amazing how much partying you can do on $74 a week. The only problem with that, of course, is that when you set those kinds of priorities, some other things have a way of going by the wayside—things like house rent, phone bill, water bill, gas bill, electric. Even at $60 a month for rent, I just couldn't seem to scrape together enough money to pay all the bills. Of course, the utility companies didn't take kindly to not being paid either. So after a while, the gas, water, and electricity were all shut off. After a couple of weeks of this, I decided I absolutely had to find a way to take care of my financial obligations.

Do you remember Pam, one of Bob's old girlfriends? Well, I was over at her house one day, and there were a bunch of guys getting ready to go somewhere—I had no idea where. Then one of them they called Renegade called over to me.

"Hey, Bud, do you wanna go?"

"I don't know," I said. "Where are you guys going?"

That he answered back: "We're headed to Clearwater, to give blood—"

Then another voice interrupted, "Plasma, man! We are giving plasma!"

Renegade shrugged. "Yeah, yeah, whatever. All I know is that they pay ten bucks a pint."

I didn't know what plasma was, but I did hear the part about the ten dollars.

Renegade looked over at me sort of strangely. "You ever done this before?" he asked. "You know...they stick a big horse needle in your arm... I was pretty sure that wouldn't bother me. After all, I was always half numb anyway."

"Hey." I shrugged. "Whatever..."

So we all hopped in the car and headed off. It was about an hour's drive, so on the way we listened to the radio, BS'd a little, and bummed cigarettes off whoever had them. All the way there I kept thinking, *Hey, they pay for giving blood? Why haven't I done this before?*

Finally, we arrived in beautiful downtown Clearwater. Actually, it wasn't all that beautiful a part of town. As a matter of fact, it was kind of dreary looking. I remember seeing a couple of winos sitting there, leaning against the walls and bumming cigarettes and whatever else they could beg—quarter dollar, half dollar. What was really funny was that I thought I was better than those guys! It's amazing how far "not being proud" will get you in life. I will say, however, there were some gorgeous ladies working in that place.

The whole process took a couple of hours, which I wasn't really expecting. First you had to fill out the necessary paperwork, and then you had your finger pricked so they could get your blood type. Then you waited while they tested your blood. The coffee was free, so we all indulged in coffee and conversation. It's amazing how the topic of conversation varies according to the beverage being shared.

After a while, one of the nurses called my name. I had been the first in line of our bunch, so I walked over to the counter and stood.

"Right arm please," she said demandingly.

I cautiously extended my right arm. She then placed a plastic band around my wrist—the type that you get in the hospital. I looked over at her. "What's that for?"

"Talk about your dumb questions! This is your ID bracelet," she said without a bit of expression in her voice. "This is to ensure that we put the right blood back into you after the process is through!"

I stared at her blankly. "Put the right blood back into me," I repeated to myself. Then I gave a sort of mental nod of my head and said to myself, "Oh well…whatever." I felt too ignorant to ask her about it, but I sort of assumed I was going to find out eventually.

"Now, sir," she said, holding out a clipboard to me. "You'll have to sign this form. We found tetanus in your blood, and this is just to acknowledge that we've informed you of this."

Once again, I found my jaw dropping. "Oh no," I replied. "What does that mean? Does that mean I'm not going to be able to give blood?" So far as I was concerned, that $10 I was going to get for this was already spent.

Then she said those beautiful words: "You've obviously had a tetanus shot recently. You'll be paid an extra two dollars for it…if you'll just sign here."

Will I sign? You bet I will! You've had thought I just won the lottery. *All right!* I thought excitedly. That makes a total of $12. I'm in the money now. The guys had already told me that you could give plasma twice a week—that was $24! I just found a part-time job!

I was just contemplating this utopia I had just found when I realized the nurse was talking to me again. "Okay, let's go." She handed me some papers and pointed me toward the elevator door. "Take these, and go on up to the second floor. Hand these papers to one of the nurses up there, and they will get you started." Then she quickly turned and called out another name.

I did as I was told and headed for the elevator, waving to my pals as I passed. Naturally, I was acting the cool dude. To tell you the truth, since this was my first time and all, I wasn't quite sure how I should act, but mainly, of course, I was thinking about the $12. What a good day it was turning out to be. So up the elevator I went, and before I had time to worry about it much, I was on the second floor. I stepped off the elevator and into a beehive of activity. There were five or six women clad in the traditional hospital white, zipping around that room, talking to each other, filling out forms, and drinking coffee. It was all pretty impressive, let me tell you.

One of the ladies approached me. "Yes, sir," she said with a smile. "Can I help you?"

All I could really do was hand her the papers. My usual charming personality was sort of on standby until I had this whole ordeal behind me. I didn't know yet how all the pieces fit together, and I was getting a tad anxious at this point. The woman looked down at the paperwork for a moment then looked up and smiled again. "Okay, follow me, sir, and I'll get you all plugged in and going."

To be truthful about the whole thing, I wasn't at all sure that I cared much for the way that she put that last statement. I went with her nonetheless. She led me over to a large archway where a two-part curtain was hanging. When I got over on the other side of that curtain, I just couldn't believe my eyes. What I saw looked like a military hospital ward from somewhere back from World War II. There must have been fifty beds in there lined up in two rows. The headboards of each were against the wall, and there was an aisle between the beds so that the person in the bed could look across the aisle and see the person in bed on the other side. All the beds were about six feet apart, and they were all occupied except for maybe two or three. I somehow knew that one of those two or three was reserved for me.

Still following the nurse, I went stolidly down that narrow path between the beds; and as I did, I could just feel the eyes following me. Some of these guys were just lying there, and some were squeezing tennis balls that were in their hands. They could probably tell that I was new here, and I'm sure that some of them must have sensed my tension as well. Just for a fleeting moment, I thought to myself, *What am I doing here?* But I really knew, of course, I was earning twelve dollars—that's what I was doing. Now for the first time, it occurred to me that maybe I'd have to earn it.

We stopped at one of the beds, and the nurse said, "Here we are, right here."

I lay down on the bed, and then another thought occurred to me. I wonder where the women's plasma center is? I could see nothing but male bodies stretched out down the corridor. That thought was soon dispelled when I saw the size of the needle the nurse was unwrapping! I couldn't hold back the "whoa, baby" that slipped unbidden from my lips. Then of course, my secret was out.

"Oh, is this your first time?" she said, looking concernedly over to me. I just nodded. "You're not feeling sick, are you?" she asked.

"No," I assured her, and I wasn't; but I sure had never known that they made needles that size. It was as big around as a metal coat hanger.

"Okay," she said as she tied a rubber tourniquet around my arm. "Make a fist, please."

I waited anxiously as she turned the shining point of that new needle around and headed it on a collision course with a vein bulging out of the inside of my arm. I'm sure that my eyes were big as silver dollars when the point was just about to touch my arm. I couldn't take it any longer. I closed my eyes and gave her a little groan. Then—how embarrassing—I felt a tear rolling down my cheek as my eyes remained closed because I didn't want to see if anyone else had seen this.

And then as soft as anything I had ever felt in my life was the soft caress of something on my cheek. I knew what it was, of course, and I also knew that the jig was up. I might as well open my eyes and as I did so saw the gentle warm smile on the face of that nurse. I suppose I'll never forget it as she softly took a tissue and wiped that tear away. She didn't say a word, but suddenly I knew that she knew that lying in front of her was just some mother's baby boy not as hard and tough as he thought he was or pretended to be. Then she got back to business again.

She handed me a tennis ball and said, "Here, squeeze this for a while until your hand gets tired. But if you want to stop and rest, just remember the more you squeeze, the quicker you'll be done."

I felt really warm inside being around this woman who had been so kind to me. On the other hand, I really didn't want to be here all day with this needle sticking in my arm, so I got to work with a passion on that ball and watched as my blood ran through that little transparent tube and into the bag. The bag was hanging on a little scale device that was weighted so that when the bag was full, it dropped down with a click.

When the bag was finally full, there was another nurse standing nearby; and when she saw the pint was finished, she came over and started clicking off the little parts on the hoses that led to the bag. Then she took a label from the paperwork that I brought with me and compared the name on it to the wristband I was wearing.

While she was doing this, I muttered in relief, "Boy! I sure am ready to get this needle out of my arm!" It was starting to hurt a little bit now.

She looked over at me quizzically. "Is this your first time here?" I was beginning to get a sinking feeling way down deep inside as I answered, "Yes."

Then she asked, "Didn't anyone explain this process to you when you came in?"

"Process?" I repeated. "What process?"

"The process we go through here," she said. Then she took a deep breath. "All right, let me explain to you how this works. First, you give us a pint of blood like you've just done. Then we take it to the lab and separate the plasma from the blood. Then we give the blood back to you along with a saline solution. Then after that is done, we go through the process one more time. After that, you'll be done. Do you understand?"

I gave a long exasperated sigh then nodded. "Yes," I said. "Yes, I understand."

So off she went to the lab with my blood, and I, for my part, just sort of lay back there on that bed, thinking of one of my dad's favorite sayings: "Nothing is ever free in this world!"

The time went by pretty slowly after that, but it did go. Finally, I was done. Oh, what a relief it was when they pulled that needle out of my arm. They made me sit up for a while to make sure that my head was still in place, then it was back down to the first floor to collect my reward. The other guys weren't quite done yet, so I sat there in the lobby for a while with a ten and two ones in my pocket with a look of satisfaction on my face.

Feeling contented with myself, I just sat there and watched guys of all sorts and ages and backgrounds walk through that place. And as I did, my feeling of contentment began to fade and was replaced by a sort of "ghost of blood banks future." I began to think about how huge and cold this world really was, and I felt as if I were about to be swallowed up by it. Was this really all that I had to look forward to in my life? Was this to be my claim to fame? Being known as the Plasma King? It was really frightening to think that I had sunk this low. I was glad, at least, that my dad wasn't around to see this, but I had this disconcerting feeling that he knew.

Then I came back to reality by the sound of Renegade's voice, saying, "Hey, Buddy, are you ready to go man?"

I was happy that someone had come along and rescued me from that dose of reality. "Definitely," I answered. Then we all went out into the parking lot and got in the car and headed off to the liquor store which was just the normal routine for these guys. Once inside the store, we all bought ourselves a couple of packs of cigarettes and then all pitched in for a case of cold Budweiser. We gave Bill, the driver of the car, a couple of dollars each for gas. I never had a chance to tell them that I made $12 instead of $10. I decided I would just keep that my little secret.

Down the highway we rolled, having a smoke and a cold beer and some of us singing along to the radio. It was party time, and suddenly the world didn't seem so cold anymore. You probably guessed that my mind wasn't anywhere close to thinking about paying the bills either!

CHAPTER 17

The next few weeks, I stayed close to home, going back and forth over to Pam's house and riding to the plasma center with the guys now twice a week. My house was now completely without any utilities, so, of course, no one wanted to live there with me. I guess I just seemed to be satisfied with hanging out at Pam's and giving plasma twice a week. I knew that sooner or later I would be hearing from the lady that I owed that rent money to.

There was a lady I knew from the bar named Anna. She had started talking about getting her daughter back. I didn't really know why she didn't have her daughter in the first place. I suppose that was none of my business. She had met a man in Gulfport they called Hoss, and they had decided after a short courtship that they would get married. Now they were on a mission to get Anna's little girl back. Her name was Jill; she was three years old. Beautiful little girl with blue eyes and blonde hair. Hoss and Anna had gotten jobs; however, they were a couple of hours away from home. They asked Pam if Jill could stay with her while they were away working. Pam agreed, and besides, she was always up for making a little extra money.

One day a few of us were over at Pam's as was the norm. We were sitting out on the front stoop of her house just talking and having a few beers. I asked one of the others where Pam had gone. One guy that was there named Ben told me that she had gone down to get Jill from a playdate with another kid. As we sat there, we could hear a child's scream from down the road a bit. It was Jill, and she was not happy at all that she had to come back to the house. She must have been having a pretty good time playing with the other kids.

Pam had a hold of her arm, and Jill kept trying to pull away. Then, with one last-ditch effort, she pulled as hard as she could and got away from Pam. Her newfound freedom had caused her to run into the street, where she was immediately struck by an oncoming car. The impact sent her flying around twenty feet through the air and down onto the pavement.

Now the sound of screaming was coming from Pam. We all looked at each other in horror, not believing what we had just seen. Then Ben ran out and picked Jill's tiny body up off the street and brought her over and laid her down on the soft grass. I had learned somewhere that you're never supposed to move an accident victim— but we could all see that it wouldn't have mattered. She was gone. We were all just standing there with blank expressions on our faces. I looked over toward the car and saw a man inside with his head in his hands, obviously not believing what had just happened. It all happened so quickly that there was probably nothing he could have done to avoid hitting her. Pam, in the meantime, had dropped to her knees and just wept. We didn't know what to do. Somebody finally had the wherewithal to call the police. We all waited there with this little girl until the ambulance came and took her away.

This was, without a doubt, the worst day of my life. I started to feel sick inside, wondering who and what we would tell Anna. I felt so sorry for that little girl, and I knew there was nothing I could do to make the situation better. I decided it was best if I just went home and got away from this tragedy. This was something that I would never forget, and I still think about it from time to time.

I walked on back to my house and just lay down on the couch, trying my best to go to sleep for a while. Finally, I did doze off for a while, then I was awakened by the sound of a car pulling in. It was my sister, the one that my mother had moved in with. She had decided to drive over and check up on me. I was really glad to see her, but I didn't talk about what had happened that day. She came in and sat for a moment then got up and looked around the house.

She came out of one of the bedrooms and questioned me. "Do you not have any electric?"

"No," I answered. "It's all been shut off. I didn't have the money to pay the bill."

She looked at me in disgust. "Get your stuff! You're coming home with me!"

I wasn't sure that I wanted to go with her, but she didn't seem to want to take no for an answer. I asked her, "Are you sure about this?"

"Well, I'm sure that you're not going to live like this!" she demanded.

So I gathered up a few of my dirty clothes and another pair of shoes that I had along with a toothbrush and some toothpaste, and off we went. I wasn't at all sure how this was going to work out, but somehow, I knew this was probably the best thing for me. I was about to start a new chapter of my life. I still wasn't in much of a talking mood, so we just drove along, smoking a cigarette and listening to the radio. Then after a couple of miles, I turned over toward her and said, "Thanks…for looking after me."

CHAPTER 18

We finally arrived at her house, and when we pulled into the driveway, I could see my mom looking out the window. I could tell by the look on her face she was glad that my sister had retrieved me from the old house. There weren't enough bedrooms for everyone, so I would be sleeping on the couch. I had been sleeping on the couch at the old house too, so that would be fine with me.

The smell of home cooking filled the room as I walked in; I had definitely missed my mom's cooking. I hadn't had a hot home-cooked meal in quite some time, and I was really looking forward to it. We had iced tea to drink with our meal, and I couldn't help but remember the last time I had drank iced tea.

It was so nice sitting around with my family at the dinner table that night. My brother-in-law asked me what I had been up to. I really wasn't in the mood to discuss my recent life and adventures.

"Oh...just trying to get by," I answered.

Then he threw another question at me; this one was a little harder to answer. "So what are you going to do now, Buddy?"

I felt like telling him that it wasn't my idea to come there in the first place! I just said, "I need to get a job, I guess."

My sister piped up. "We might be able to help you with that," she said. She had been talking to another one of my sisters and found out that they had built a new Sheraton Hotel on Sand Key. They were looking for help to move all the furniture into the hotel. Turned out my other sister knew some people down there and had already landed the job for me if I wanted it. The only problem was it was quite a ways from this house, and I really didn't have any way to get there. After I lost the keys to my car in my near drowning, I found out that it was too expensive for me to fix. So I just sold it for a couple of hundred bucks.

Anyway, they all agreed that they would help me get back on my feet. My brother-in-law said I could probably find a cheap apartment in Clearwater, not far from the hotel, and he would loan me his bicycle to get to work. I told them that I would take the job and I really appreciated their willingness to help me out.

A few days later, we found a one-bedroom apartment for $30 a week. I thought to myself, *Man, that's twice what I was paying before—or at least what I was supposed to be paying.*

The place was in pretty bad shape, but at least it was cheap. It had everything I needed even though the bathroom was pretty nasty. My mom came over before I moved in and spent probably a couple of hours scrubbing the bathroom on her hands and knees. You know what they say about a mother's love—it's endless.

I took the job and started a few days after I moved into my apartment. I knew this part of Clearwater. It was only a few blocks from the plasma center. That was one place I decided I wasn't going back to anymore. My arms were full of holes now from all the needles they had stuck in me.

I guess I was really in need of some exercise because when I started riding that bike, it was killer; but after a week or so, it became a lot easier—actually a lot of fun. I was making enough money to pay my rent and buy groceries. Now I was eating regular meals that I cooked myself. It seemed I was starting to turn my life around.

On my route back and forth to work, I noticed there was a car lot with a big sign that said PAY BY THE WEEK. So one afternoon, on my way home from work, I stopped in to see if I could possibly afford a car. The man at the car lot was more than willing to work with me and my limited funds. Payday was on Friday, and I told him I would be back on Saturday to get my '65 Buick LeSabre—a really cool car back in those days. When I went back on Saturday to sign the paperwork, I noticed I was getting charged 11 percent interest. I asked the man why he charged so much.

He responded by saying, "Look, man, I don't know you from Adam. I'm the one taking all the risks here. So you take this car out, and a month later you total it. Then you call me up and tell me to 'stick it.' There's nothing I can do. I've just lost a car!"

"Well," I said. "I hadn't really planned on totaling the car, but I will take it nonetheless."

Those big V-8's they had back in the sixties really packed a punch. This Buick would get up and fly! White on the outside and light-brown leather on the inside—it was actually really nice—and it even had an AM radio. I figured somewhere down the road I would have to install an eight-track tape player.

Anyway, I loaded the bicycle in the trunk and took off for my sister's house to return it.

My brother-in-law commented, "Looks like you're starting to get it together, Buddy."

"Yeah, I think you're right," I told him. "Thanks for the use of the bicycle."

By this time at the hotel, all the furniture was in place, and everything was set up and ready for business. I landed a job as the nighttime bellhop, working four to midnight. I was working seven nights a week because we were still a little shorthanded. I didn't make as much per hour, but I did pretty well in tips. Not as much as the dayshift, of course, but I was doing all right. I wouldn't get home till around 12:30 a.m. I would usually just go straight to bed then sleep in the next day. It was nice not having to get up early to go to work, and I was really enjoying myself in my new life. My drinking and partying now were almost nonexistent.

One day I had a few hours before I had to leave for work. It was a beautiful day outside. I decided I would walk around the block and check out the neighborhood—something I hadn't done yet. On my way down the road, I noticed some young kids playing with a ball in their yard. I was probably a hundred feet from them when I saw their ball roll out into the street. One of the younger boys jumped up and ran toward the street to retrieve his ball. As I looked around, I saw a car coming in the other direction.

Instantly, without thinking, I just started screaming as loud as I could possibly scream: *"No! No! No!"* It was so loud, in fact, that the little boy and the car both stopped in their tracks. The memory of Jill came flooding back to me as I stood there watching. Thank God this had ended well. Now my heart was pounding, and I just turned around and headed for home. *Maybe I had scared that little boy*, I thought. *I sure hope so.*

As the days passed, I wasn't at home very much. I had taken another job at the hotel, driving the shuttle bus during the day. I was still working the night shift as a bellhop too, so they gave me a room to stay in at night. I thought that was nice of them. Now I was basically living at the hotel. It was fun. During the day I drove for eight hours and at night helped people check in and get their luggage up to their rooms. I asked if I could make dinner reservations for them or anything else they needed to just let me know. The guests normally stayed for at least three to four days, so I would pass a lot of them walking around the lobbies or in some of the restaurants. They always spoke to me, asked me how I was doing, then we would have a short conversation. I was getting to be well known among the guests, and I really enjoyed it.

Then one evening, as I was sitting at the bellhop desk, the manager of the hotel came up and said he needed to speak with me.

I said, "Sure! What's on your mind?"

Then he dropped a bomb on me! "Buddy," he said. "I see you around during the day, talking to the guests. I don't want you bothering the guests anymore."

I tried to explain to him that I wasn't bothering the guests, but I was just talking to them. I told him that most of the time it was the guests that started the conversation with me.

Then he repeated what he had first told me: "I don't want you talking to the guests! Do I make myself clear?"

I just shook my head in disbelief. "Yeah, I understand."

This crushed me—and what was I supposed to do if the guests came up and asked me something? Was I just supposed to ignore them because of the marching orders I had just been given? I was getting madder and madder by the second, but what could I do?

I decided I needed some time away from this place. I decided that tomorrow, I would go over to the secretary's office and tell her I needed the weekend off because I hadn't had any time off in a long time, and I needed a break.

"What about the shuttle?" she asked.

My response was not very nice: "I guess you'll have to find someone else, won't you? Anyway, I won't be here Saturday or Sunday."\

She looked at me in disbelief, for I had never been mean-spirited toward her. "Buddy, is there something bothering you? Are you all right?"

Then I realized what I had done, speaking to her so harshly. "Look," I said. "I'm sorry. I just need the weekend off, okay?"

"Okay," she said. "I'll work something out."

After my shift ended on Friday night, I decided to go back to my apartment. I already knew what I was going to do on Saturday. I was going to head back to Gulfport and party with my friends. I really needed this—or so I thought. Saturday afternoon came soon enough, and I got into my Buick and headed south. I had still been in a bit of a funk Saturday morning, thinking about what the manager had told me. I thought, *Maybe I'll just find another job?*

Why not? I thought. *I have transportation now. I don't have to ride a bicycle to get where I'm going!*

I pulled into the Rocks' parking lot, and before I could get out of the car, another friend of mine named Jimmy came up to the window.

"Hey, Bud! Where you been, man? I haven't seen you for a while?"

"Yeah," I answered. "I'm living up in Clearwater now and working a lot of hours at the Sheraton. I decided to take the weekend off. So what's going on?"

"Well," he said. "Me and George rented a hotel room at the Holiday Inn in Saint Pete. We're gonna party over there tonight. We got a room right next to the pool. I just came back here to recruit some people. So whatcha say, do you want to go?"

It took me about two seconds to ponder my answer. "Hell yes, I want to go!"

"Well, that's good," he answered. "Because I need a ride back over there. Where did you get this car anyway? It looks really nice!"

"Yeah," I answered. "I've had it about a month."

So off we went, headed for the hotel and for what I thought would be a great night! We stopped off at a 7-Eleven to get some beer and wine; of course, I hadn't eaten since breakfast at around nine that morning. When we got to the room, there were a couple of people inside the room and four or five more sitting in the loungers around the pool. Jimmy went into the room and came back out holding a fifth of Southern Comfort, which later would be known to me as "sudden discomfort." So now we were drinking shots and chasing them with beer. This continued on until around 9:00 p.m. Then Jimmy asked if I could give him a ride back to the bar. I agreed, so off we went. Of course, I had no business driving a car. Regardless, we made it back to the Rocks and went inside. Lo and behold, the first person I spotted was Dawn, sitting at the bar, looking at me. I must have been drunk because I walked right over and gave her a big hug.

"How you doin', baby?" I slurred.

Was it my imagination, or was she hugging me back very tightly? I had obviously forgotten everything from our past relationship. I sat down next to her, and we started talking just like old times. I told her that I was living in Clearwater and working up there at a hotel.

She looked at me concernedly. "You're not thinking about driving back there tonight, are you? Not in your condition!" Then she held my hand softly in hers and said, "Why don't you stay with me tonight? I have a little apartment just down the road from here. We could actually walk there."

"Okay," I said. "I'll do that!"

So we sat there for a while, talking and having a couple more beers, which I definitely did not need at that point. Then something came up—I can't really recall what it was, but she started arguing with me about it. Then for a couple of minutes, we argued back and forth, then she said, "You can forget about staying at my house tonight!"

"Fine!" I said. "I'll just drive home."

Bad decision! I finished my beer, got up, and soloed out of the bar. I staggered around outside the bar for a while because I had forgotten where I was parked. Eventually, I found my car, got in, and started her up. I would say my apartment was roughly thirty miles away. Have you ever heard the old expression "most accidents happen within a mile of the house"? This bode true for me as well because I was about a mile from the apartment when I passed out at the wheel.

I was driving down a four-lane boulevard, speed limit fifty. I'm sure I was doing at least sixty. I found out later from a newspaper article that there had been a witness not far from the scene of the accident. My car veered off the road, hitting the curb, bouncing up, hitting an old wooden telephone pole. The impact split the pole in half, then the car went flying right through a huge plate glass window and landed on the showroom floor of a GE appliance store. I had no idea what had happened; I was still passed out at the wheel. It wasn't until the police got there and an officer reached over, grabbed my right arm, and started pulling me out of the car that I regained consciousness. The pain was excruciating in my right shoulder, but everything else seemed to be okay. Now I started looking around at all the washers, dryers, refrigerators and the like that were scattered around on the floor in front of me. I thought I was in a dream; I definitely didn't know how I had gotten here.

He yanked me out of the car, still clutching my right arm. I started yelling a bit because it hurt so bad. He pushed me up against the car, grabbing my arms, putting them behind me, and cuffing me. We walked through the debris outside to the squad car where he started pushing me into the backseat.

I shouted at him, "I need to go to the hospital!"

He answered back, "You're not going anywhere but jail, you idiot!"

True to his word, he took me to the county jail, where I was photographed and fingerprinted. Now my right shoulder was really beginning to ache. Something was definitely wrong if it hurt this bad even with all the alcohol that was in me.

He left the handcuffs on me through this whole process, and it wasn't until he opened the door to the drunk tank that he removed the cuffs. Without saying a word, he closed the door and walked away.

I turned back toward the door, looking through the little window, and started yelling, "Officer, officer, please take me to the hospital!"

It became obvious at that point that I was not going to the hospital. I would just have to tough it out at this point. I turned around and saw that the cell was about twenty feet long and about the same distance wide. All around the border of that room were old wooden Coca-Cola flats placed upside down. I suppose they didn't want to make it really comfortable for the drunks that would be spending time in there. I noticed one other man sitting across the room from the door. He was speaking quite loudly, but he wasn't speaking to me. Every once in a while, he would yell out, "I don't belong here! Let me out of here!"

After about ten minutes of hearing this speech of his, I finally stood up and walked over to where he was. I said, "Look, dude, I don't know why you're in here, but I'm really tired of listening to you yell!"

Well, my threatening him seemed to work, or maybe he was just tired of yelling. Or maybe at that point, he realized that it wasn't doing him any good. Anyway, I welcomed the quiet. After a while, my bladder was telling me that I needed to go to the bathroom.

Instead of beating on the door for the officer in charge, I decided to ask my new friend, "What do you do when you have to pee?"

"At this." He pointed to a small drain in the middle of the floor.

I asked him again, "Are you kidding me?"

"No," he said, shaking his head. "That's where you go."

Oh wow, I thought. *When in Rome!*

After that, I did manage to doze off after a while. I have to say that sleeping on those wooden flats was definitely not comfortable. At least the first time I spent the night in jail, I had a bunk to sleep on. Oh yeah, I forgot to mention that this was my second time spending the night in jail. That time, it wasn't my fault though. No really, it wasn't.

One night, I had stopped in Dickie Doo's to see who was in there, and I saw another old friend named Toby. He stood up to greet me when he saw me and almost fell down. He was so drunk. I convinced him to let me drive him home and managed to get his car keys from him. I put my arm around him and managed to get him out to the car, opening the back door and basically pouring him into the back seat. Then, I got in the front and started the car.

I pulled out onto the road and went maybe four or five blocks when I saw police lights flashing behind me. I couldn't understand this because I was within the speed limit. I checked, and my lights were on. So the next available spot, I pulled over into a parking lot, turned off the car, and waited for the policeman to come up to my car.

It turned out to be Officer Ben, known to all the locals as Big Ben, because he was, as I said, *big!* I rolled my window down; and when he came up to the door, I looked at him sort of puzzled and said, "Ben, what the hell? I wasn't doing anything wrong, man!"

He looked at me then and said, "When was the last time you checked your license tag?"

I told him I never checked it because it wasn't my car. I pointed to the back seat at Toby and said, "I'm doing a good deed. I'm driving this drunk home because in his condition, he probably would've killed somebody if he would've drove."

Well I guess he wasn't in a very good mood that night because he went ahead and wrote out a ticket anyway. He said, "When you go to court, tell the judge your sob story, and maybe he will go easy on you."

"Yeah…thanks a lot, Ben!" I responded.

Anyway, it was about four days before I had to appear in traffic court. I was down at the Rocks as usual on a Saturday night when Toby walked in. He walked up to me and said, "Hey buddy, I went down to the cop shop to pay your fine, but I was five dollars short. If you could loan me that five dollars, I'll go back and pay the fine and then you won't have to go to court."

So I loaned him the five dollars, then forgot all about my date with the judge. I figured it would all be taken care of. The middle of the next week, I was at the Snack Bar. I had just come in after work for a beer. I hadn't even had the first sip of my beer when someone tapped me on the shoulder. I turned around to see Big Ben and Sergeant Frank standing behind me. Frank looked at me with a happy smile on his face and said, "Buddy, I have a warrant for your arrest for failure to appear in court."

I told him I didn't have to go as that fine was already paid. He just shook his head and said, "No, how are you going to pay your fine when you didn't go to court."

Now I knew what had happened. Toby hadn't paid any fine. He just wanted five dollars from me to get a drink somewhere. I looked at Sergeant Frank and asked, "Is it okay if I drink my beer first?" He agreed and stood there as I finished my beer.

Then he asked me, "Do we need to put handcuffs on you?"

"No!" I said. "You should know me better than that."

Anyway, they took me down to the station and booked me and put me in jail. Some friends of mine came in about a half hour after they had booked me and wanted to bail me out. The officer told them they couldn't do that because I had been drunk and disorderly, which was just a big lie. After sitting in that cell for around twenty-four hours, an officer came in and said I could have a phone call.

Well, of course I had to call my mother and ask if someone could come and get me out of jail. I dialed her number and waited patiently for someone to answer the phone, then in a flash, it hit me. Oh no! Today is mom's birthday! I just felt sick when she answered the phone. I wished her happy birthday and then had to tell her what was going on. It felt good though, telling her that it was all just a misunderstanding and that I hadn't broken any laws. So that was the first time I had spent the night in jail. This time, however, it was definitely my fault.

I knew for sure that I did not ever want to be in this situation again! I managed to arrange my arm in a position that my shoulder didn't hurt quite as much. I woke the next morning to the sound of the officer telling me it was time for my phone call.

Now came the worst part! I would have to call my mom because that's the only number I knew.

When she answered the phone, I just blurted out, "I'm in Clearwater Jail. Can you come and get me?"

She wanted to ask me twenty questions, but I stopped her short and said, "Mom, can you just come get me please!"

Now she and my sister both heard on the news about a car driving through an appliance store showroom. They didn't associate that with me, but I think they probably had their suspicions. My sister came in and paid my bail while my mother waited in the car. I could tell she was very disappointed in me because she never said a word. I could also tell by the way she was looking at me that she wasn't really happy.

As we walked through the doors to the outside of the building, she asked me where my car was.

Sadly, I answered her, "I guess I don't know? I was in an accident last night."

"Oh my god!" she gasped. "Are you the guy that drove into that store last night?"

"Yeah, that was me," I answered, being disgusted with myself.

As we walked toward the car, she noticed that I was holding up my arm with my other hand. Holding my arm close to my chest seemed to be the best place for it.

Then she asked, "Are you all right?"

I shook my head. "No, there's something wrong with my shoulder."

Now she was mad at me. "Dammit, Buddy! When are you ever going to learn? You're really lucky you didn't kill yourself! So what happened to your shoulder? Did you tell the cops you were hurt?"

"Yeah, I did, but they didn't seem to want to listen. I told the one cop last night that I needed to go to the hospital. He said I was going to jail. He didn't seem too concerned with the pain that I was in."

"So now what!" she fired back. "Do I have to take you to the hospital too!"

She had a right to be mad at me, but I was starting to get a little upset with her attitude toward my injury.

"Look," I said. "Just take me home if it's not too much trouble."

We got to the car. Mom turned around and managed a little smile for me but never said a word. I just had a sick feeling inside of me.

We started across the parking lot toward the road, and my sister told her, "Yeah, that was him that ran into that store last night."

My mother just sighed and shook her head. I guess neither one of us knew what to say at that point. I knew I had messed up big time. My sister was right—even though my shoulder hurt, I was lucky to be alive.

When I got to the apartment, I gobbled down a few aspirins, trying to relieve the pain, but it didn't have much effect. Later that night, I went across the street to use my landlord's phone. I called my mom and told her of the pain and that I really needed to go to the hospital. She called one of my cousins, and he came and got me. After getting to the emergency room, they took an x-ray of my shoulder and determined that it had been separated. They were able to pop it back into place and gave me a sling to wear for a few weeks along with some painkillers.

The next day, of course, was Monday, and I was expected to be back at work. I decided I would walk all the way to the hotel to let them know what had happened. When I entered the door, a few of the people that knew me gathered around to ask what had happened. I didn't tell them the whole truth. I just made up a little story that wouldn't put me in such a bad light. I looked up and saw the manager approaching me.

He walked up and asked me, "So...did you enjoy your time off?"

I could tell he was upset about that too. "Well," I said. "I'm going to be in this sling for a little while, so I probably won't be real good at carrying suitcases, but I'll still be able to drive the shuttle bus."

"No," he said. "We found someone else to do that job. Actually, Buddy, you left us in a real bind. Don't bother coming back. I'll have my secretary write up a check for you. Sorry!"

I'm sure he wasn't sorry. I really don't think he liked me all that much to start with, but I was the one that screwed up. I had no one to blame but myself. When would I learn, as my sister had asked? Now I didn't have a job or a car. I wouldn't be able to afford my little apartment anymore either.

Something good did happen to me in the midst of all this—if you can call it good. Before I went to court, my mother found a lawyer that would go to court with me for the low cost of $100. We met in her office a week before I had to appear before the judge. I told her everything that happened and that the officer refused to take me to the hospital for treatment. When she heard this, her eyes lit up.

She repeated, "Did you say the officer refused to take you to the hospital?"

"Yeah," I answered.

"Wow...don't worry about a thing," she assured me.

The day of my court appearance came. I was sitting outside the courtroom on a bench, waiting for my attorney. When I finally did see her, she came over and sat down next to me.

"I have good news," she said. "The case has been dismissed."

I was shocked. "What!" I said. "We haven't even gone into the courtroom yet."

Then she said, "There's no need for that. I went back to the judges' chambers, told him what had happened, and threatened a lawsuit against the city. When the judge heard that I was denied medical care and that we had just cause for the lawsuit, he decided to drop the charges and let me walk—and walk I did!

Now I had to call the man in the car lot and tell him what happened. It had been a month like he had mentioned in his explanation about the high interest rate. "Yep," I told him. "I totaled it!"

I never saw the car, but my mom and sister did. My mom said it was a miracle that I lived through it! Then she actually said if I hadn't been so drunk I probably would have gotten hurt a lot worse? Mom, if I hadn't been drunk, there wouldn't have been an accident!

I suppose it was a miracle. God was definitely looking after me. I could have died from the overdose of pills. I was definitely drowning in the bay that night, and now this accident left me with nothing but a separated shoulder. I can't even remember if I was wearing a seatbelt that night. My future wasn't looking real bright right about now, but at least I was alive. I had enough money from my last check to pay for a couple more weeks' rent while I tried my best to find another job—within walking distance, that is.

CHAPTER 19

I wasn't having much luck finding another job, and as I sat at my kitchen table, looking through the want ads, a car pulled into my driveway. I got up and looked out the window. It was my cousin Bob. He had heard through the family tree what had happened to me and came by to see how I was doing. I told him I only had a few days left on my rent and my money was running low. I told him I wasn't really sure what I was going to do. I would not go back to my sister's house after all they had done and me letting them down. He said he understood that, of course, and offered me the couch at his house. Well, that sounded good to me because my prospects were not looking very good.

So I gathered up all my stuff and moved in with my cousin, who was now married with two stepsons. He said he would pay me a little bit if I wanted to take care of his yard work and a little bit of painting that he wanted to be done in his house. That sounded good; it gets pretty depressing not having a little money in your pocket.

One of his neighbors saw me mowing the lawn and came over and asked if I would be interested in doing their lawn too. After that, a couple more mowing jobs followed. Then after that, his wife and I decided to start a lawn service. We called it "Cousins Lawn Service." We even printed up business cards, and on the bottom of the card, we wrote, "We do relatively good work!" She was going to school at the time to become a nurse, so I did most of the work. That meant that I was pocketing more of the money. My cousin would let me borrow his car from time to time so I could go into Gulfport and see the old gang once in a while.

None of my friends had heard about the accident, and I decided I would keep it that way. One night, as I was driving toward the Rocks, I passed the topless bar and saw Dawn walking in the door. As it happened, she saw me too. We just stared at each other for a few seconds, then she went inside, and I headed on toward the bar. I really didn't see anybody I knew, so I just grabbed a stool at the bar and ordered a beer. I figured sooner or later somebody I knew would come in. There was an older lady sitting next to me that I had never met, but after a few beers, we struck up a conversation, talking about whatever.

Then suddenly, out of nowhere, there was Dawn standing behind me. She said she wanted to talk to me.

I thought to myself, *Oh no, not again!*

At this, the lady that was sitting next to me asked, "Do you need me to get up?"

"No, no," I said insistently. "You stay right there." Then I turned and asked Dawn, "What do you want?"

I couldn't believe what she said next. "Buddy… I love you… marry me and take me away from all this!"

I felt like I was on a candid camera. Then I looked at her in disbelief. "Did you really just say that to me? As I recall…you're already married! And why aren't you at work right now?"

Then she whined, "I don't wanna work there anymore. I don't want to do that. Please, Buddy, just listen to me!"

"Dawn," I said. "That is never going to happen. Just leave me alone."

She just became more insistent that I talk to her.

I kept telling her, "No, no! Just leave me alone, please!"

Well, then it became apparent that she was not going to leave me alone. So I got up off my stool and headed out the door, not really knowing where I was going. I decided to cross the street and walk down the pier. As I did this, Dawn was following me just a few feet behind. As I got about halfway down the pier, I could hear her yelling at me to please stop. So I did as she asked and stopped, leaning up against the side of the pier.

"Look," I said. "I am not marrying anybody! What brought all this on anyway? The last time I saw you, we were having an argument…and now you wanna marry me? Look, I'm going back to the bar. Please…don't follow me!"

So now I headed back down the pier toward the bars. I decided not to go back to the Rocks but next door to a bar called the Snack Bar, another place that I often visited. As I reached the door, I turned around to see that she was once again coming toward me—except this time she was about a hundred feet away. I didn't know if she was going to follow me in here or not, but I knew I was done talking with her.

After I entered the Snack Bar, I walked down to the end of the bar and just stood, kinda bending my head to see out the window.

Then I heard a female voice say, "Are you looking for someone?"

I turned toward the voice to see this redheaded lady that I had seen in there before. I didn't know anything about her, not even her name. I told her I was kind of looking for someone—someone that I really didn't want to see.

She seemed puzzled. "Why is that?" she asked.

"It's a really long story, but I wonder if you would consider doing me a favor."

"Sure," she said. "What's the favor?"

"Well…" I answered. "This is gonna sound kind of weird, but there might be a girl coming in here in a few seconds. If she does, would you be willing to lay a big kiss on me? I think that might deter her."

"Sure," she agreed. "Just let me know when."

And at just that moment, as I had figured, Dawn walked through the door, looking for me. I looked at the red-headed lady and said, "Now!"

Our lips came together in what seemed like a two-minute lip lock. I opened one of my eyes to see if Dawn had left, and sure enough, my plan had worked.

Our lips parted. She looked at me and asked, "Did it work?"

I just nodded and said, 'Yeah, great job!" I thanked her and then turned to walk away.

She grabbed ahold of my shoulder and said, "Hey, what's your hurry?"

Oh, I thought. "Nothing, I guess."

So I walked back and stood next to this red-headed lady. Enter Sally! She told me her name, and then I told her mine.

"Yeah," she said. "I've seen you around."

I couldn't have known at this point that I was talking to my future wife.

One thing led to another, and before I knew it, she and I were living together. She had a good job with the local power company, and I didn't have a job. She didn't seem to mind that, though, and was supporting me. This seemed okay to me for a while, but eventually, I knew I had to hold up my end of the bargain.

One day, I decided to go back over to my cousin's and see what was going on with him. He informed me that he and a friend had been laid off that week. They were seriously considering going to Houston to find work because at that time the city was booming. He asked me if I wanted to go with him. I told him I probably should, seeing as how I wasn't doing any good there in Florida. I decided that I would go. I had Sally's car, so I had to go pick her up from work that evening. I told her I had good news and bad news.

She said, "Just tell me!"

"Well," I said. "I'm going to work! But I have to go to Houston to do it."

She wasn't really happy about it. In fact, she told me that if I went, our relationship would be over. I told her I was sorry she felt that way, but I knew that I had to go.

At that, she got really mad. She told me to pack my clothes and just go to my cousin's now!

"Okay," I said. "I'll do that."

So I called Bob and asked him if he could come pick me up. I started packing my things, which didn't amount to much. So now, I ended up back at my cousin's house, which was fine with me because we were leaving in just a few days to go to Texas. The more I thought about going to Houston, the more excited I got. Work was very plentiful there, and I really needed to get back on my feet.

I had told some of my friends in Gulfport that I would be leaving, and they decided to throw me a going-away party the night before I left. I really wouldn't have expected any less from them. We would be leaving for Houston early on a Saturday morning, so the party was set for Friday night. We started out at the Rocks, of course, then over to a girl named Dottie's house. The party went on into the early morning. At about 3:30 a.m., I told Dottie I needed to get a ride over to my cousin's house. He had told me they would be leaving at 5:00 a.m., and if I wasn't there, they would leave without me.

She agreed to give me a ride. It would take about a half hour to get over there, so I figured I still had plenty of time. I didn't get to leave right away, however, because of people hugging me, saying bye, telling me they would miss me, and so on. So by the time we arrived at his house, it was going on 4:30 a.m. We would be traveling in a pickup truck with a cap on the back. So I took all my worldly belongings, which amounted to one grocery bag full of dirty clothes, a carton of cigarettes, and a five-dollar bill. I opened up the back of the truck and saw that Bob and his friend had already stowed their stuff. I threw mine in where there was room. There was also a mattress in the back with a pillow and blankets for the trip. I had drunk quite a bit that night, so I figured instead of going in the house, I would just go ahead and crawl in the back of the truck and close the lid behind me.

I laid down on the mattress with my head on the pillow and pulled the blanket over me.

I thought to myself, *This is pretty comfortable!*

It only took a couple of minutes, and I was sound asleep. It was so early in the morning that it was still dark out. True to their words, they came out of the house at 5:00 a.m., got in the truck, and took off for Houston. My cousin told me later that he and his friend—I later learned his name was Alex—decided that I wasn't coming and never saw me lying in the back of the truck. I slept for a couple of hours, and by then it was pretty much light outside when I woke up. I could feel that the truck was moving, so I decided to raise up and get a look out the window. Upon doing this, Alex, who was driving and seeing me in the rearview mirror, practically drove off the road.

I guess that could freak a person out! Then right away, my cousin whipped his head around to see me grinning from ear to ear and giving him a little wave. He just shook his head in disbelief. We drove a few more miles down the road, and then we pulled into a gas station. I crawled out of the back and went around to where my cousin was. He tried to pull a trick on me and asked what I thought of Texas.

I looked around and then answered, "Oh, I didn't know Texas had palm trees?"

Bob then told me the reason for leaving so early that morning. He wanted to make it to New Orleans by that evening to visit his old friend, Reverend William Wesley. He was a black preacher that had taken Bob in when he had been down in the dumps and had turned into a drunk, with no direction in his life. I was anxious to meet the Reverend because now, I was in the same situation Bob had been in when he first met him.

While at the gas station, we filled up and grabbed some snacks for the road. Now it was Alex's turn to hop in the back for some rest. Bob drove, and I rode shotgun. It was really nice because he and I were both sober at this point. That hadn't happened that often in the past couple of years. We talked about our life. We talked about family. He was laying out his plans for when we got to Houston. He figured the three of us could work together and subcontract some carpentry work. He was a carpenter, I was basically a carpenter's helper, and Alex was a crane operator. So I guess he was gonna learn a new trade.

At long last, we reached New Orleans. Bob knew exactly where he was going. He pulled up in front of the house where the Wesleys resided. It was in an old neighborhood. There were a lot of ramshackle houses around, but this house seemed to be in pretty good shape. He said we could spend a couple of nights there. We could spend tomorrow wandering around New Orleans and then hit the road early Monday morning.

I just looked at him and said, "Hey, man, I'm just here for the beer!"

The three of us got out of the truck, walked up on the front porch, and knocked on the door. Mrs. Wesley answered the door with a telephone on the side of her head attached to a very long phone cord on which she was having a conversation with her husband.

When she saw the three of us standing there, she paused on the phone, and the first words she said back to the phone was "Bob's back!" Then she paused again then said, "I've got three white faces standing here. Whatcha want me to do with 'em?" Then she said. "What? I'm not gonna dance with 'em? You know white boys ain't got no rhythm!"

Hearing this made us all break out laughing, and now I was feeling more and more welcome at this house. Then she walked back in toward the house and hung up the phone. She came out on the front porch through the screen door and gave Bob a big hug. "So," she said. "I see you're still alive!"

She told us to get back in our truck and follow her over to a house where the Reverend was working hanging sheetrock. She said we could help him work on the house and she would go back and cook us up some dinner, as she put it. Following this woman was quite the experience. I don't know if everyone in New Orleans drove like she did, but she definitely owned the road. She was driving an old gold Cadillac, and every stop sign that came up, she would just slow down a little and lie on her horn. Now Alex was back in the driver's seat, just shaking his head in disbelief, as he tried to follow her through that crowded neighborhood.

We finally—and safely—made it to the house where the reverend was working.

Mrs. Wesley pointed to the front door and said, "Go on in. I'm going back to the house."

The reverend was happy to see Bob and gave him a big hug as his wife had done. The reverend said it was good to see us because he had some heavy work to do and could use our backs. There really wasn't that much left to do, but we were happy to help. We finished hanging the rock and helped the reverend clean up and gather his tools and then headed back to the house.

When we walked in the front door of that house, I could smell that Mrs. Wesley had been busy cooking. Boy, did it smell good! We all walked in, and upon seeing us, she told us to sit down at the dining room table. Meanwhile, the reverend had washed his hands and gone to the back room then reappeared with a cold beer for all of us. Mrs. Wesley sat all the food down on the table like we used to do back in the day. It was fried chicken, mashed potatoes, gravy, biscuits, and some kind of greens.

She then instructed, "Now if you boys eat all your food, I got a big peach cobbler for dessert that I made earlier. I knew I wouldn't have a problem cleaning my plate; all I had to eat that day was some cheese crackers and a Pepsi. Now I was thinking I must surely have died and gone to heaven. This was some of the best food I had ever eaten in my life! We all ate our fill and talked, getting to know each other, and—oh, that peach cobbler!

Now supper was over, and our bellies were full. We all got up from the table and followed the reverend to the back room, where he had earlier gotten the beer. I walked into the room to discover a pool table sitting in the middle of it and an old refrigerator off to the side where the beer was obviously stored. So for the next couple of hours, we shot pool and drank beer. It was just like being back at the bar except there was no jukebox. After a while, we decided that we had better get to bed after our long day on the road.

I was sleeping like a log on an old single bed that they had in another room in the house when Bob came in and jostled me to get up.

"Wake up," he said. "Time for breakfast!"

Once again, I woke up to the smell of something wonderful cooking. Mrs. Wesley had outdone herself again. There were eggs, sausage patties, bacon, grits, and more of those big biscuits with plenty of butter that we had for supper the night before. The coffee smelled awesome! I thanked her and told her I was sure going to miss her cooking. The coffee pot was sitting in the middle of the table, and I had a cup already set out at my place. I made the comment that the coffee sure smelled good then took the pot by the handle and poured myself a cup. I added a little cream and sugar, then while I was stirring, I noticed everyone seemed to be looking at me.

Okay, I thought, never expecting what would happen next. I took a sip of the coffee, then my eyes got as big as the saucer my cup was sitting on. I swallowed, then catching my breath, I said, "Man, that is some strong coffee!" The others at the table were all laughing at me now.

Then my cousin said, "I guess you've never tasted chicory coffee before?"

"What?" I answered. "Chick what?

Then the reverend chimed in, "Chicory, son, that's Louisiana chicory coffee! That's the only kind we drink in New Orleans! Put a little more cream in there, that'll make it taste better to you."

I did what the reverend told me to do and added much more cream. I pushed my cup aside then and filled my plate with this wonderful food that Mrs. Wesley had prepared. Again, it was delicious. I was surely eating well for a poor man. Then I managed to finish my coffee and even had one more—with lots of cream!

After breakfast, we all sat around out on the porch and talked while smoking our first cigarette of the day. Bob was planning on taking us on a tour of New Orleans—starting with the French quarter. It wasn't really much of a tour; it basically consisted of four bars and a bunch more beer. After that, we headed back to the reverend's house, and I guess he had given his wife the night off because we decided to order pizzas for dinner—and more beer, of course. We played some more pool, and then decided we had better get to bed because we had an early start in the morning. We planned on hitting the road by seven.

Mrs. Wesley had told us the night before, "Sorry, boys, I don't get up that early!"

I made sure to thank her and tell her what a great cook I thought she was. She appreciated that.

The morning came, and we were all up, having more chicory coffee. We said our goodbyes, got back in the truck, and headed toward our final destination. Alex had decided to climb in the back and get some more sleep, so Bob drove, and I rode shotgun. We made it to the city limits of Houston around one thirty and pulled into a convenience store. I filled up the truck while Bob went to get a newspaper. He was looking for someplace cheap for us to stay while we found work. We were fortunate enough to find a furnished

one-bedroom apartment for $75 a week. It had everything we need-
ed—a kitchen, a bedroom with two beds, a couch, one chair, dishes,
pots and pans, and even a television. Bob and Alex would take the
beds, and I would sleep on the couch. We were right off Interstate
610. We would sit on the front walkway and watch all the traffic go
by. The neighborhood was mostly made up of Mexican people; this
was a first for me, but they were nice and very accepting of us. This,
of course, was my first time living in a big city like Houston. We
could look out the front window and see all the high-rises downtown.

That afternoon, we just sat around and took it easy. Alex had
met another man that had moved to Houston from New York, looking for work. He told him about a section of town where they were
building a bunch of apartments and needed help. So we decided early
the next morning that's where we would head. True to the stranger's
word, we found job site after job site with HELP WANTED signs. This
was crazy! I had never seen anything like this before. We pulled into
one of the sites and parked over by a job trailer. We all got out. Bob
went in by himself. He was only in there about five minutes when he
came back out with another man that was pointing over to the back
corner of the site.

He came back to the truck with a smile on his face. "Well,
boys," he said. "Looks like we've got a job!"

Bob had contracted out to put roof trusses on one of the two-
story buildings that were there. The buildings were all going to have
flat roofs, so it probably wouldn't be that hard. We drove over to
the building and parked. While Alex and I got out all of our tools,
Bob set off on foot to find a forklift driver to bring us our trusses.
It seemed like forever before that driver got to us with our material.
We just patiently waited and looked at the blueprint that Bob had
gotten from the foreman. He wanted to make sure we all understood
what we were doing. When our trusses finally got to us, we only had
time to get them up on the walls and sort of spread them out, but not
really put any of them in place. We decided we would get here early
the next day and finish the job.

The next day came, and we busied ourselves getting all the
trusses installed. We had all the big ones in place, then there were

some shorter ones that were to overhang the entry porch on the front of the building. Bob decided he would climb out on these trusses to finish them up and put some trim pieces in place. Then tragedy struck. Bob fell off one of the trusses all the way to the ground, breaking his collarbone.

The foreman called an ambulance, and they took him to a nearby hospital. We could not believe what had just happened. Alex and I picked up our tools and made our way to the hospital where they had taken Bob. On our way back to our apartment, Bob said that we would go and finish the job the next day; he would tell us what needed to be done, and we could finish it. We couldn't collect our check until the job was finished. We would have to take some of our earnings and buy him a plane ticket back home. Alex and I decided to stay in Houston, not really sure what we were going to do.

Alex took Bob to the airport later that evening. I chose to just stay at the apartment. I would get a newspaper and start looking for something to do. Now there were two people looking for work and only one mode of transportation. On his way home from the airport, Alex had stopped at our neighborhood watering hole for a couple of beers. He had been talking to a man that told him that there was a temporary labor pool not far from us. He said we could go and work over there and make $20 a day. It was called Casey's Helpers, right across the street from the Salvation Army. A lot of the guys that worked for Casey were staying at the Salvation Army. In other words, they were in a little worse shape than I was at the time. Alex and I decided we would check this place out and see if we could make a little money to survive while we looked for something else to do.

We would get there before seven in the morning—you know, first come first served. That way we would surely get a job for the day. They also had free coffee and donuts every morning, so that was a plus. There were some real characters working there. I'll never forget one morning looking around and seeing this man walking toward the table where the coffee and donuts were. He was wearing a really nice suit.

I thought to myself, *What are you doing here?* Then I looked down and saw that he was barefoot, and his feet were very dirty. I just chuckled to myself. I thought, *Well, you look good as long as nobody checks out your feet!*

We did all sorts of odd jobs. They had a van that would take us to the job then pick us up in the afternoon and bring us back to Casey's. I did such things as unloading carpet pads from semitrailers, unloading frozen french fries from a railroad car. One day I was at a scrapyard separating steel and aluminum from huge piles of metal. Before we started, the foreman warned us to look out for rats hiding in the piles then handed us a pair of leather gloves. This kind of freaked me out, but at least he warned us, right! They even went down to the local burger joint at lunch and bought food for us. I thought that was nice. Separating metal was really hard and dirty, but at one point during the day, I thought to myself, *At least I was making more here than I was giving plasma.*

After Bob had gotten hurt, I decided to write a letter to Sally, telling her what had happened. I didn't give her our location, but apparently, she was smart enough to see the return address on the envelope. One day after returning from work at Casey's, I was in the parking lot of our apartment building, talking to some kid that was playing down there. All of a sudden, I hear a voice yell, "Hey, you leave that kid alone!"

I turned around and, to my surprise, saw Sally walking toward me. She had packed up, quit her job, and decided to join me in Houston. I couldn't believe it! Here I was once again in a bad situation, and another woman would save me from this desperate place that I was in.

CHAPTER 20

It was a great reunion—she and I together again. We continued to live at that apartment for a couple of weeks while I kept working at Casey's. Meanwhile, Sally looked for a job and an apartment for just the two of us. Alex, meanwhile, was seriously considering going back to Florida. I suppose she and I could have stayed at that apartment, but we figured we could find somewhere a little less expensive. So that's what we did—found our own place—and Alex went home.

Our new digs were unfurnished, of course, so Sally bought us the basics with the savings she had brought with her. I went back into the electrical field as an apprentice once again, now making twice what I was making at Casey's. After a couple of weeks, Sally managed to find a job as well. So now the two of us were working and making money. Things, once again, were looking up for me. The electrical contractor that I was working for was only a mile from our apartment. Sally would drop me off in the morning and then head off to her job. Then I would walk home after work. I was starting to really feel good about myself once again.

One afternoon, when I got back to the shop after work, as we were pulling in, I saw Sally parked on the side of the road, waiting for me.

I wondered, *Why is she there so early? Hopefully, she hadn't lost her job.*

Anyway, I got out of the truck and went into the shop, as was customary, to get my assignment for the next day. Then I headed out to meet her. She greeted me with a warm smile as I went around to get into the passenger side.

"So," I said. "Why are you here?"

"Well," she said. "I have some news for you."

"Okay," I answered. "Good or bad news?"

"Oh, I think it's good news." Then she just turned and looked me square in the eyes and blurted it out: "I'm pregnant!"

I just froze, not really knowing how to answer her announcement. All I could think to say was "Really?"

She said she had taken off work early that day to see a doctor and confirm that she was, in fact, pregnant. At this time in our lives, Sally was thirty-seven, and I was just twenty-four. She looked at me with enthusiasm in her eyes and asked, "Well, what do you think?"

I paused for a few seconds and then managed to spit out the words, "Am I old enough to be a dad?"

She laughed at my unexpected remark and said, "Don't worry, you'll be a year older when the baby is born."

Well, now, I supposed it was time to give her a big hug and kiss and tell her this was great news. *Wow*, I thought. *Now things are really going to get real.*

As was customary back in my day, I, of course, would ask Sally to marry me. That's just the way it would be. I would do the responsible thing—marry Sally and become a parent. I was pretty sure I wasn't ready for this role, but I knew I had to get ready. We continued working hard and saving as much money as we could to prepare for the new addition to our family.

Sally looked like she had swallowed a basketball the day we got married. We got hitched at the local courthouse, accompanied by a friend of mine from work and his wife and one other guy from work that, when he heard about the wedding, demanded that he get to come. He said if I invited him, he would buy our dinner. So, of course, I let him come. He could also busy himself by taking some pictures with our old Polaroid camera. I think he managed to get a couple of shots before the camera quit working. Then right in the middle of the service, he spoke up loudly, "Hey, what's wrong with this stupid camera?" At that point, I thought it would have been better if I would have just bought my own wedding dinner.

Now, within the course of a little over six months, I had gone from being destitute, without any real hope in my life, to leaving my home in Florida and moving to a place totally unfamiliar to me and now married, with a baby on the way! Before Sally had come to Texas, I really didn't know where my life was heading; but now, it was pretty well mapped out for me. I would work hard and try to be the best husband and father I could be.

I'll never forget the day we brought our newborn home from the hospital. As we were walking up the stairs to our second-floor apartment, I noticed two men in suits standing at our door—two Jehovah's Witnesses wanting to talk to us. After I informed them that we were just bringing our child home from the hospital, they were very generous and decided we were probably too busy to talk to them. I thanked them, and they went on their way.

So now here we were, the three of us as a family. Sally took a leave from work, and I continued working hard. After the baby came, I approached my boss about maybe getting a raise. I explained the situation to him, and he generously gave me a fifty-cent raise. That would surely help out because we were working eight hours of overtime every week as well.

We were getting tired of apartment living, so after a while, Sally found a little one-bedroom house in the country for the same rent we were paying before. This was nice because now we had a decent-sized yard and a front porch to sit out on. Out in the back of the property, there were two rental trailers, and next door was another house. After a bit, we got to know our neighbors and made new friends. We had our own little community. The only downside was the distance from work. It was about fifteen miles away, but I had the car, so it wasn't that bad, I guess.

I had to be really careful driving because I had lost my license after my accident. They had dropped the DUI charge that would have meant jail time, but they suspended my license for a year. I decided I needed some sort of identification, so I went down to the license bureau to get a Texas ID so I could cash my checks at the bank. I told the woman there that I had lost my license somewhere. I hadn't even thought of trying to get another driver's license. The woman asked me where I was from. I told her the truth—sort of. I told her I was from Ohio, which was where I was born. I told her I had a valid license before I lost it, which was also true in a sense. Of course, this was back before the days of computer networks, so she handed me some paperwork, I filled it out, answering all the questions correctly, and got a Texas driver's license.

Boy, I thought. *That was easy!* Now I had a job, a wife, a baby, and a driver's license! Could things get any better!

As time went on, I loved my baby girl more and more, but it seemed that Sally and I were starting to grow apart. I was at work five days a week, which left her at home with the baby. This was okay for a while, but soon she began to grow restless. She decided she would look for work and we would find a sitter for our daughter. This, of course, meant we would have to find another car. Sally had gotten a job, and it was quite a ways away from the house. She said we needed to find somewhere to live that was closer. So now it was back to apartment living for us, and I really missed our little house and the privacy that we had there.

It turned out to be very noisy in our apartment, seeing how we were on the first floor and the people above us were very loud. This really got on my nerves—so bad that it also affected my relationship with Sally. It seemed as if we were arguing every day more and more now about things that really didn't matter at all. We decided we needed to get out of this apartment and find one on the second floor that would be quieter for us. So we moved once more, into a place that was much quieter, but the arguing didn't seem to stop. Our feelings for each other were starting to diminish—almost to the point where I could probably say that we really didn't like each other much.

One day, I got home from work, walked into the apartment to find that she had moved everything out, including my baby girl. Everything was gone except for my clothes. It was like I had walked into the wrong place. I could not believe that she had done this. My heart was in my throat, and I started to cry. I had no idea where she had gone to. Now here I stood in this empty apartment—no place to sit down, not a bed to sleep in, not even a glass for a drink of water. I walked over to the refrigerator and opened it. To my surprise, there was my beer and my lunch meat for work. So I cracked open a beer, walked down, and sat by the pool, drinking my beer while smoking a cigarette. At this point I was lost and wondering just what it was I was going to do now. I had no idea where they had gone to or even whom to ask.

The one thing I had enjoyed was getting home every evening to see my little girl—now she was gone. I had never known where Sally was actually working, so I couldn't look there for her either. Three weeks passed, and I was gradually getting things for my apartment.

There was a new kid at work that had come from Alabama and was sleeping in his car until he could afford a place. I told him he could come stay with me and split the rent if he wanted. His name was Cooper, and he jumped at the chance to get out of his present accommodations. I had bought a single bed at a resale shop, and Cooper had a sleeping bag and pillow, which seemed just fine to him. A week later, we went together and bought a couch at the same resale shop that I had found my bed. At that point, he decided the couch would be more comfortable than the floor.

Now it had been five weeks since I had come home to an empty apartment. Then one Saturday morning, as I was sitting on the couch, drinking coffee, a knock came on the door. I couldn't believe it—it was Sally and my baby. I was still really mad at her for what she had done but also super excited to see my child. Cooper was offered some overtime on that Saturday, so he had gone to work, so it was just me that morning. I knew for the sake of my baby I had to control my temper and just play nice. It was wonderful holding her again.

Sally cautiously asked, "Is it okay if I come in?"

I paused then said, "I guess?"

Then, as if she was completely oblivious to what she had done to me, she asked, "Is that coffee I smell?" followed by, "Do you mind if I get a cup?"

All I had were paper cups, but I told her, "Go ahead and help yourself."

Then she came back out and sat next to me on the couch. She did her best to apologize to me for what had happened, but I wasn't buying any of it.

She said, "I guess I was just mad at you because of all the fighting we were doing, and I really didn't want to live like that."

I wasn't doing any talking, just listening and enjoying my daughter's company.

Then she said she thought that we should really stay together and try to work things out then told me where she was living and said, if I was so inclined, to please stop over. Anytime would be fine with her.

I still wasn't talking much, but I told her I would think about it. I certainly did not want to revisit what she did to me just five weeks ago.

They stayed about another half hour, and then she announced she had to get going, once again telling me to stop over if I wanted to. I really wanted to spend more time with my daughter, so I asked if she could stay a little while longer. What I meant was that I wanted my daughter to stay longer, but she could leave anytime. I knew better than to say something like that—surely it would just start another fight.

True to my word, the following week went by, and I did think about stopping by her new address. So Friday after I got off work, I went home and cleaned up then went over to see her. Maybe I could give it another try—for the sake of my baby, of course. When Sally and I weren't fighting, we actually had a lot of fun together. Maybe this time it would work. Driving down the street that she was living on, I was surprised that I didn't see any apartment buildings. As I approached the number that she gave me, I gazed upon a nice-looking house. I thought to myself, *This couldn't be it…could it?*

As I was pulling into the driveway, Sally came out the front door to meet me. She seemed happy to see me. She was all smiles.

"Hey, you're just in time," she said.

I stopped and bought a pizza for dinner, and the beer was cold. I responded, "Yeah, I could eat!"

So we walked into the house together, and as I entered, I couldn't help but feel that she wanted me to move in so she could afford the rent. This place was awesome! Three bedrooms, two baths, dining room, living room, family room, and a nice-size fenced-in backyard.

Then she turned to me and asked, "So what do you think?"

"I think it's great," I answered.

"Yeah," she returned. It belongs to a guy that I work with, and he let me have it for $400 a month—which was a little more than we were used to paying for apartment living. It's a little expensive for just me." Then she smiled coyly. "But together it wouldn't be bad at all." Then she got a serious look on her face and asked, "I sure hope you've decided to move back in with us!"

I didn't like the tone of her voice at all, so I replied, "You know, Sally, I'm not the one that moved out!"

After I said it, I knew it would surely create more fighting between us; but strangely enough, it didn't. She walked up to me and hugged me really tight and apologized for what she had done then asked me if I could ever forgive her. I could not believe these words were coming out of her mouth. It took me by surprise so much that I actually forgave her. Then we kissed! This really felt good, but in the back of my mind, I was wondering, *How long would this last?*

Then we decided to eat the pizza before it got cold and have a couple of beers. It turned out to be a great evening, sitting there, eating pizza with my daughter on my knee—felt like old times again. Maybe all we needed for this marriage was to get out of apartment living and into a nice house like this one. I told Sally that I would move back in, and we would try our best to be a family again. So I ended up staying all night, playing with my baby, and later making love to my wife. I had convinced myself that this marriage was going to work.

CHAPTER 21

Saturday morning came, and I drove back over to the apartment to tell Cooper of my plans. I told him he could keep my bed and the couch but that going back to my family was what I felt I had to do. He didn't seem to be too upset, saying maybe he could find someone else to help share the rent with him. So I headed over to the grocery store to see if I could find some boxes to put my stuff in. After I scored some boxes, I was back to the apartment to pack up my stuff. I filled the boxes, carried them down, put them in the car, and off I headed back to the house. I felt I was happy with the way things were going. I guess I was still a little uncertain how it would all work out.

Months passed, and we seemed to be doing pretty well, but we were getting bored because we really didn't have any social life. I had some friends at work, and she did also. We felt we needed to get out and do some things without our kid sometimes, so we found a reliable sitter and started going out on Friday nights. This seemed to help the relationship quite a bit. Then after a while, we started to want a little bit more of social life, so we decided that one of us could go out on Saturday night alone as long as we let the other person know ahead of time.

The next week at work, one of my coworkers invited me to his birthday party. He said it was going to be on this coming Saturday night. I told him I could probably come; I would just have to let my wife know. I let Sally know about the party on a Wednesday night, so this was adequate enough time in advance, I figured. She said that was fine, and I should plan on going.

So finally, Saturday rolled around. I had been working out in the yard all day, so now it was time to clean up to go to the party. As I entered the house, I mentioned to Sally that I was going to get a shower before I went to the party. She had a look of uncertainty on her face, so I reminded her, "You remember the guy at work invited me to his birthday party tonight, right?"

"Oh...yeah, I guess I had forgotten," she said.

"Well," I answered back. "I haven't forgotten about it. I'm not sure what time I'll be home, so don't wait up for me." Then I proceeded on to the shower and then to the bedroom to get dressed.

It was now time to leave, so I gave my baby and Sally a hug and kiss goodbye and headed for the door. I got in my car, started it up, and started backing down the driveway. All of a sudden, I heard a loud bang on my car. It sounded like I had backed into something. I looked back toward the hood of my car and, to my disbelief, saw Sally on the hood of my car, hanging onto the windshield wipers. She was yelling at me, "You're not going anywhere! You're not going to any party!"

I could not believe it! I put it in park and got out and just stood by the side of the car. I could not believe this was happening!

I looked at her then and said as calmly as I could, "What the hell are you doing? We agreed on this! Come on," I said. "Get off of my car. You're going to end up getting hurt." Then I reached over and grabbed her around the waist to try and pull her off, but she would not let go. I tried to take her hands off the windshield wipers, but she just tightened her grip on them all the more. To make matters worse, now the neighbors across the street were looking at us and starting to wonder what was going on. The last thing I wanted was for this to turn into a major incident, so I reached back inside the car, turned it off, put the keys in my pocket, and started walking down the road.

After I was a couple of blocks away, I turned to see if Sally was following me. She wasn't, so I guess she figured now that I was walking, she had won the battle. So now I just stuck my thumb out and started hitchhiking. I finally made it to the party—a little bit late, of course. I told my friend I had to walk over because I had some car trouble then asked him if maybe I could get a ride home later. He said he would be happy to do that for me. That was good because I definitely didn't want to hitchhike back.

It was a nice party, but along about midnight, things started to die down. I asked my friend if he could give me a ride home then.

"Sure," he said. "Let's go."

When we arrived at the house, I got out and thanked him. He drove away, and I walked toward the house. As I neared the front door, I reached out to turn the handle, and wouldn't you know it, the door was locked. So I walked around to the back of the house and tried to open the sliding glass door. It was also locked. Now I couldn't get into the house.

Did she do this on purpose, or just out of habit? I wondered.

So I walked around to the bedroom window. I tap lightly on the glass and called her name. I know she had to have heard me, but she wasn't budging. Now I was starting to get mad because I figured she had done this on purpose for whatever reason. I walked around the house now, checking the other windows. Luckily, I found one that I could open and got back into the house. Now I was inside, and I was fuming. I decided it would probably just be best to sleep on the couch and calm down, but first I would have another beer to help curve my emotions. As I sat there, I did manage to calm down as I thought to myself, *I guess I really should have had a key to the front door with me.*

The next morning came, and I tried to talk to Sally about what had happened the night before. She was in a mood and refused to talk to me about anything. I couldn't understand why she was so mad. I mean, after all, we had a discussion about this weeks before. If my memory serves me, I remember her agreeing to this arrangement—of us going out alone with prior notice—but I just couldn't seem to get through to her. I guess we would just have to agree to disagree—at least we weren't fighting although I think the silent treatment was even worse than the yelling.

On the Friday of the next week of work, I was finishing up on a new house. I was sitting cross-legged on the floor, making the electrical connections to a dishwasher. When I was finished and I went to stand back up again, a loud pop came from my knee and echoed through the house—so loud, in fact, my apprentice who was in the back bedroom came out and asked what the noise was that he had heard. I told him I thought it was my knee, but I really wasn't in any pain! I didn't feel any pain then, but when I woke up Saturday morning, it was a whole different story. When I got out of bed, I found that I couldn't put any weight on that leg, and the pain was getting worse by the minute.

Sally asked me what was wrong with me when I hobbled into the kitchen. I told her the story of what had happened to me the day before. Apparently, after my knee popped, it had been a delayed reaction until the pain started. Either that, or the way I had slept on it caused it to start hurting. I took some aspirin and decided to tough it out. If it was still bothering me by Monday morning, I would tell the boss what had happened and ask to see a doctor about it.

Monday morning came, and my knee still was not any better. So I made it to work and limped into the office to talk to the owner. I told him what had happened on Friday and that my apprentice was also there and heard the pop. He told me that he believed my story and told me to go to the emergency room to get it looked at. After they took x-rays, a doctor came in and told me that I had a severely torn meniscus cartilage and that I would need surgery to remove it. I was a little unsure about all this because I had never had surgery before. The doctor assured me that surgery was the only way to fix it. They left me in the exam room for a while.

Then about fifteen minutes later, the same doctor came in and said, "We have you scheduled for surgery next Monday."

Of course, they wanted to know if it was a job-related accident then had me fill out a bunch of paperwork. He said their office would contact my employer to verify my employment with the company. Then he said, "Be sure, and stay off of that leg."

The good news was that Workmen's Compensation would pay for everything and even send me a weekly stipend till I was able to return to work. At least I wouldn't be broke. When I got back home, Sally had already taken our little girl to the babysitter, and she had gone to work. So my news would have to wait until later this afternoon.

Now there was nothing I could do but follow the doctor's orders. I would just sit around, watch a little TV, maybe listen to some music, and try to get some sleep. I decided I would have dinner ready when Sally and my baby got home. I keep saying "my baby," but she had just turned two years old a couple of weeks before. When they arrived home, I was sitting in the living room, but the food was prepared for them.

Sally came in, took a deep sniff, and said, "Did you cook?"

"Yeah," I said, slowly raising myself up off the couch.

Then she looked at me again and asked, "Did you go to work today?"

"Kind of," I answered her. "First I went to work and talked to my boss about my knee, and he sent me to the emergency room. They took x-rays and told me I needed to have surgery on my knee for a torn cartilage."

"Oh no," she's gasped. "How long will you be off work?"

"I don't know," I told her. "A few weeks, I guess?" I was quickly tiring of this conversation. I said, "Hey, why don't we just eat dinner? We can talk about this later."

She agreed, and we all sat down to eat.

After we finished dinner, we got everything cleaned up. I helped as much as my knee would allow me. Sally told me just to go sit down and she would finish cleaning up. So I went on in and turned on the TV, propping my leg up on the couch. It wasn't long before she joined me in the living room. Not much was being said as we sat there.

I finally looked at her and said, "You know…my mom has been wanting to come for a visit. Maybe this would be a good time? I'll be laid up, and she can help out around the house. I'm sure she wouldn't mind helping out."

Sally didn't say anything right away and then responded, "I'll have to think about that?" I could tell by the mood that she was in that I should probably just keep my mouth shut and not question her. But then I said, "Well…don't wait too long!" Then nothing more was said.

The next morning came, and we decided not to take our little girl to daycare; she could stay home with me for now. That was okay with me, of course, with my work schedule, the way it had been, I hadn't gotten to spend much time with her especially one on one. She loved books, so we read a lot, watched some kid shows on TV, and had our lunch together. Then it was time for her afternoon nap. While she was napping, I would go into the kitchen and look around for something for supper. Surely Sally would appreciate that.

Things were going along pretty smoothly up until Friday afternoon. Sally had gotten home from work and was not in a very good mood. She must've had a bad day at the office. I suggested that we order a pizza for dinner so we wouldn't have to cook or clean up.

Then she looked at me with a disgusted look on her face and snapped, "I don't want a pizza for dinner!" Then she added, "What have you been doing all day?"

"You know what I've been doing," I said. I've been home with the baby all day and nursing my sore knee.

"In other words," she said, "you've been lying around the house all day while I was out working! And I don't want your mother coming here either!"

I just looked at her with disbelief on my face. "What the hell is your problem!" I bellowed. "You know I've been at the house all day and there isn't all that much I can do. Besides that, there is not that much that needs doing here. The house is clean! The baby's clean! You know I'm having surgery on Monday morning. Where the hell do you get off coming in here yelling at me like this?" I was starting to get so mad, then I realized I needed to get out of there for a while. I hobbled into the kitchen and grabbed my keys.

Upon doing this, she roared, "Where do you think you're going!"

I snapped back at her, "I don't really know where I'm going, but I know I'm not staying here and listening to this crap anymore."

She shouted back at me, "Leave then…go ahead and have your damned surgery…and don't bother coming back here."

I just looked at her, shaking my head, not believing what she had just said. "Don't worry, bitch!" I fired back at her. "I won't be back!"

CHAPTER 22

I got in my car and headed out, not really sure where to go. So I decided to drive over to my friend Roy's house to see if he was at home. He was always good for a cold beer and some conversation. I parked my car and went up to his apartment and knocked.

He answered the door and said, "Buddy...come on in, man."

I was glad to see that he was in a good mood. This would probably help my mood.

"Come on in," he said. "And have a beer with me."

As we sat, of course, he asked what was going on with me, and I told him the whole story. I said I was having the surgery on Monday morning, but I really didn't want to go back home. Of course, he offered me a place to stay for a few days, and you know the rest of the story. This is where my story began.

So fast forward—I spent a long afternoon in the hospital that Sunday. Right before my eyes were about to shut for the night, a nurse came in and informed me that my surgery has been moved to 1:00 p.m. I figured that would be okay until she informed me that I wouldn't be able to have anything to eat or drink in the morning except for water. That was a bummer!

The next morning arrived, and the time had finally arrived for them to wheel me down to the operating room. I was a little nervous, I guess. I had never had surgery before. My doctor assured me I had nothing to worry about. He told me they were going to put me under, and I would wake up when it was all over.

"You'll sleep like a baby," he said jokingly. He wasn't lying either—I was out like a light.

When the surgery was over and I got back to my room and the drugs wore off, I was in a lot of pain. The nurses saw to it that I had pills to take care of that.

I lay in bed the rest of the day, and the following morning, a woman I had never seen before came into my room and announced, "I am the physical therapist. I will be working with you today."

"That's great," I said. "I'm ready to get out of this bed."

"No, no," she said. "We'll be doing some exercises while you're lying down."

So for the next two days, that's what we did, and I was only allowed to get up and go to the bathroom with the help of one of the nurses.

It was Friday morning when the doctor finally came in and told me that I would be able to go home today. I had been practicing walking around the room on my crutches, and I felt pretty confident on them. After the doctor walked out, I thought about what he had just told me—that I could go home.

Where is home exactly? I thought.

All of a sudden, I was feeling really scared. "Where would I go?" I asked myself. I had told Sally that I wouldn't come back, and when I said that, I meant it. Now Roy and Connie were tired of me staying there. What would I do? I felt so lost, my head was spinning, and I hadn't felt scared like this in a long time. I called Roy to tell him I was getting out of the hospital and could he come and pick me up. He told me he couldn't do it, but his friend Jonnie could come over and get me. I told him that would be fine and I would be outside in about a half hour, waiting for him.

I gathered up what few things I had and sat on the bed, waiting for the nurse. She arrived, pushing a wheelchair, instructing me to get in. So I did what she said, grabbed my bag and my crutches, and settled in for my ride out of this building. She pushed me to the elevator, then down to the first floor heading toward the back of the hospital. I remember there was a long sidewalk that went out to a small driveway, and beyond that was a large empty field, a little bit of grass, and a lot of weeds.

Then she asked me, "Is someone coming to pick you up?"

"Yes," I said. "He's on his way."

"Well, I'll have to stay with you until he gets here," she spoke softly.

We waited there for about ten minutes, chatting back and forth a little.

Then she asked again, "Are you sure you have a ride coming? I can't stay out here with you forever."

"I'll give you permission to leave if you'd like," I answered her. "I'm sure he'll be here pretty soon."

"Okay," she assured me. "But I'm going to check back on you in a few minutes."

So here I was, all alone, waiting for a ride, sitting in a wheelchair, holding crutches, and really no place to go. I stared out into that open field. Now the world was feeling really cold again. I wondered to myself what I was going to do now. It was like living back at that house in Florida with no electricity and no hope for the future. This time was a little different though. I did have a car and a job. I wouldn't have enough money to get my own place. So what would I do?

About that time, I saw a car approaching. It was Jonnie. He finally made it. I guess I was glad to see him. With all these mixed emotions swirling through my brain, I really didn't know. We greeted each other. It was apparent to me that he had been drinking. He asked me where we were going, and I told him back over to Roy's house because that was where my car was parked. On the way over to Roy's, it dawned on me that I could go pick up my last paycheck at work. This made me feel a little bit better, knowing I would at least have some money in my pocket.

We got to my car, and Jonnie helped me out with my crutches. I thanked him for coming to pick me up. Then I got in my car and headed off to gather my last paycheck. When I walked into the office, I told the secretary why I was there.

"Oh yeah," she said. "We need to have a current address for you for your Workmen's Compensation checks. They'll be coming in next week."

I thought to myself, *Oh man, what address could I give?*

Confused, I looked at her and said, "Would it be okay if the checks came here?"

"Well… I suppose they could. Then you just wanna come by and pick them up?" she asked.

"Sure," I answered. That'll also give me a reason to get out of the house.

I went to the bank and cashed my check, and as I left, I could barely fight the urge to go and see my little girl. That was what I really wanted to do now, but I just couldn't bring myself to go back to that house—not after that huge blowout Sally and I had had. Instead of that, I headed over to Yank's Tavern, the local hangout, to have a few beers. I was driving a station wagon at the time, and I figured if nothing else, I could sleep in my car. So that's what I did. Of course, having a few beers helped me to get to sleep. I had a prescription for pain pills, but I didn't know if I wanted to fill it or not. This would be a first for me—sleeping in a car. I guess I had a roof over my head though.

As it turned out, I would only have to do this for a week. When I went to get my Workmen's Comp check the next Friday, I ran into a guy at work that I was pretty friendly with. We talked for a while. He asked me what was going on with my leg. I laid the whole long tragic story on him. When I told him I was sleeping in my car, he piped up.

"Hey, man, I need to find a place myself. I've been staying with my son and his fiancée, but I can tell that they're getting kind of tired of me being there. If you want, maybe we can go together to an apartment."

His name was Lester, but everyone called him Peewee—that was his nickname. He was older than I was by about fifteen years, but that was okay. We seemed to get along pretty well. He had a bed that he brought over, and I went down to the Goodwill and bought a mattress and some blankets for myself. I was starting all over again—again! Peewee would go to work during the day, and I would drink beer and hang out by the pool. I did, however, go back to the house and get some clothes for myself while Sally was at work. Three days a week I would go to the hospital for more physical therapy. After about three weeks of this, I gave the crutches back; I was able to walk normally again. So, of course, this would mean I would be going back to work. That felt good!

Now the weeks rolled by. I was working steadily and was able to add a few more things to the apartment. Sally and I had a court date for our divorce. I was going over to see my baby girl every Saturday for a few hours. By this time, Sally had moved out of the house and into another apartment that was more affordable for her.

I was hanging out at Yank's Tavern every Friday and Saturday night now and was starting to make quite a few friends. I met a few ladies but nothing serious. I really didn't want any relationships right now. I was more than happy just to party and hang out with my friends, which sounds exactly like what I was doing before I met Sally or before I moved to Houston. I guess some things never change.

They were starting to have live music at Yank's on the weekends, and the owner gave me the job of checking IDs and taking a two-dollar cover charge at the door. One night, I was working the door when out of nowhere walked this beautiful young lady. She had permed curly brown hair and the most beautiful brown eyes I had ever seen. She didn't look like she was twenty-one, so I asked to see her ID.

"Oh yeah," she said playfully. "Let me see your ID."

So with this, we struck up a conversation. She said she was going to have a birthday party the following week and invited me to come over.

"Well," I said. "I never turn down a party."

The party was scheduled for the following Friday night, and I was there. She was even more beautiful than she was the night we had met. It appeared that she wanted to get to know me better, and that was okay with me. I definitely wanted to get to know her better. I had completely forgotten about my past relationships. So we drank, we talked, we slow danced together to Willie Nelson music and kissed. We kissed all night long. After a short courtship, we ended up moving in together, and two years later, we were married. That was thirty-eight years ago—and I'm happy to say that we are still together today.

CHAPTER 23

We were still living in Houston, still partying, both working and doing well. By this time, Sally had met another man and had remarried. He seemed to be a pretty good guy. I had seen pictures of him and my daughter riding around on a tractor together. They seemed to be happy. I was visiting my daughter less and less, which over the years has made me feel terribly guilty. When we decided to get married, we drove to Michigan for me to meet her parents. They lived in a place that was referred to as a village. It was small, no traffic; they rolled the sidewalks up at nine at night. After living in Houston for seven years, I was really enjoying the atmosphere of this little town. We decided we would get married up there and eventually move there as well.

One summer I got a letter from Sally, saying that she would like to send my daughter up to visit for a couple of weeks. My wife and I agreed that this would be nice—for her to come and visit. I was very excited about it. After she arrived, she handed me a letter from her mother. It said that she wanted my daughter to stay with me. I couldn't believe her words! She said that she and her new husband would now be on the road driving a semitruck. So now the two weeks would end up turning into a year. We did the best we could, but it was a big adjustment for us.

After that year was up, my daughter got a letter from her mother, saying that she wanted her to come home. She told her she would have her own room with a telephone and a television just for her. It was a hard thing for me to do, but I had to tell her that she had to make a decision. Did she want to live with me or her mother?

I told her she had to choose, which was a pretty hard thing to lay on a nine-year-old kid. After a couple of days of thinking about it, she said she wanted to go home again. In the back of my mind, I knew that this was probably the last time I would see her. I couldn't have her bouncing back and forth, not knowing what her mother would do. Tears filled my eyes as I watched her walk up the stairs to the airplane. I will surely miss her.

I had met some of my wife's old friends when we first moved to Michigan, and the party had somewhat continued. Nothing at all, though, like the partying I had done in Gulfport and Houston. Was I getting bored of this lifestyle—or was I just growing up? After five years of marriage, we finally decided that we were tiring of the party scene.

One day she approached me and out of the blue said, "Let's have some kids."

That really surprised me because before she had said she didn't want to have any kids. Of course, this sent me back to thinking about my daughter. "Are you serious?" I asked her.

She replied, "Sure, I think we should."

So that's what we did. She gave me two beautiful daughters, and those two daughters together gave us eight beautiful grandchildren.

Before our children were born, we started to attend a church that one of her friends was a member of. He invited us to come one Sunday, and we decided to go. Both of our daughters were born in those years when we attended that church. It really felt good being back in church again after all those years of absence. I knew this would please my mother. I got involved in the church and actually became a deacon. After three years were up, I then became an elder of the church. I became the chairman of the Christian education committee and even started singing again in what we called the contemporary choir. I started making new friends in the church and was involved in things related to the church—none of which included going to bars.

After our girls had gotten a little older, we realized there wasn't much for them to do in this church, so we started attending a different one that had a large body of children. My two girls came away from this with a lot of good-quality friends. I joined the praise team there and played the bass for ten years. My wife was getting involved in the youth ministry and helping out with the very large youth group.

I felt as if I had finally arrived. Now I had a family, a mortgage, of course, and my wife and I were working hard to secure our future. After our kids were grown up, my wife and I started going to another church. The one that we left started having some problems that we didn't agree with. But every Sunday we are still in God's house worshiping. I am no longer the big party person even though I still enjoy a cold beer now and then. The parties we have now are usually with our family and maybe a few good friends.

As I look back on my life now, I realize I wasted a lot of good years. I could've done so much better. But as they say, hindsight is always twenty-twenty. I thank God every day for getting me through those years and saving me more than once. God was definitely hearing my mother's prayers.

When my mother turned eighty, I and my four sisters were all there to celebrate with her. She told us the most alarming thing. She said now that she was eighty, she was going to stop praying for us because she knew we were capable of praying for ourselves. But somehow, I don't think she actually quit.

I've gone back to Florida a few times for different reasons—vacation, class reunions, and, sadly, my mom's funeral. Every time I've been there, I always make a trip to Gulfport. Was I looking for my old friends? Did I just want to relive some of those days? One of those trips I actually got together with Lurch. He was still living there. I met him at his house, and it was a very heartfelt reunion. We had both survived, and now, where once was a couple of mixed-up young men stood just a couple of old men. He told me if he knew he was going to live that long, he would have taken better care of himself. I had to agree with him on that point. We decided to go for a beer down at the Rocks. We went in and sat down at the bar. I, for one, just couldn't believe I was sitting here again next to my friend. We sat there as if no time had even passed in our lives—having a couple of beers and reminiscing about the dumb things we had done in our youth.

Eventually, I was back home with my family again, feeling safe and secure with the life that I had made for myself. It was fun being back in Gulfport, but I knew that it wasn't my Gulfport anymore. It had changed quite a bit from the days of my youth—now a much-sought-after place to live. Yeah, there are still quite a few bars, but a whole new younger crowd had taken our places, and I was okay with that.

Now the years have tumbled along, and I'm an old grandpa. I love my family, and I thank God every day for the life that he gave me. Maybe he knew I had to go through rough times to get here. If that's the case, I thank him for that as well.

Now at the ripe old age of sixty-seven, as I was sitting in my living room, browsing on Facebook, I see a message come up. It was from my firstborn. It had been thirty-three years since we were together. I couldn't believe it. I was really happy to be in communication again. We started texting back and forth, and I decided I would go and visit. I was thrilled to hear that two of my sisters, one of my nieces, and her boyfriend also wanted to come. It was a grand reunion. I was with my child again, hugging, accompanied by a few tears. All of my sisters, my daughters, nieces, nephews are all very welcoming. They are all communicating through social media. Alone for quite a few years, now there's a new member in the family, and we are loving it. I'm sure God had something to do with this as well.

This book has taken a long time in the making, and after I retired, I knew I had to finish it. All I know is for some reason, I felt I had to tell this story. I guess there's more I could say, but I suppose I've said enough. All I can tell you is this—put your faith in God, look for him with your heart and not your brain. He's there—just give him a chance. Read the Bible, learn what Jesus did for you—his sacrifice—because he loved us. We all have a life to live, and granted, there will be some bumps along the way. Just try to learn from your mistakes, and do your best.

A while back, someone posted on Facebook. The scene was a beautiful lake with trees, flowers, and greenery all around. At the edge of the lake was a small bench, probably just enough room for two people. The caption said, "If you could sit on this bench for an hour, and talk to anyone, dead or alive, who would you choose?" Without really thinking, I put the name of Jesus in the comment box.

Wouldn't that be incredible? To sit and talk to the Savior of the world. Would I actually have enough nerve to do that? I would probably be more calm sitting at his feet. Then what would I say? Thank you? I love you?

He would most likely tell me to get up and sit next to him. Maybe he would ask me, "Why are you so afraid?" I probably would not be able to find the words. I imagine he would calm me and tell me not to be afraid. He might say, "Buddy, I hope you know that I have always been by your side, watching over you. I have heard all of your Mother's prayers, and I hope you know how much she loved you."

Hearing this, I would surely start to cry. I would answer him, a little calmer now, "I know she did, Jesus. I know she did. I also know that I must have surely hurt her throughout my life, never intentionally but just by some of the decisions I made."

We would sit, enjoy the scenery and talk in bits and pieces. I can imagine him looking at me and saying, "Buddy, our time is almost over. Is there anything else you would like to say?"

Then, just one thing would come to mind. "Jesus, I would ask. There is one thing I would like to know as the tears would no doubt start to flow again. Was it you that saved me from drowning that night?

He would probably smile slowly and look at me and say, "It wasn't your time, Buddy. It just wasn't your time." Then, he would be gone.

I would stay there for a bit longer, wondering, *Did this just happen?* I could only imagine.

ABOUT THE AUTHOR

Buddy is a retired electrician from a small village in Michigan. He was born in Ohio, moved to Florida when he was eight years old, grew up there not wanting to do anything but play baseball. He moved to Texas in 1976 and then on to Michigan in 1983. He became a member of the Edwardsburg Presbyterian Church, where he served as deacon and elder for six years. He coached soccer for thirteen years in a local recreational league and also travel soccer. His family left the Presbyterian church and started attending the local missionary church, where he played bass guitar with the worship band for ten years. He attended Southwestern Michigan College and also M-Tech at Lake Michigan College. He is also a member of the local Lions Club. Now he spends most of his time working on his ten acres, gardening, and lawn care.

CPSIA information can be obtained
at www.ICGtesting.com
Printed in the USA
JSHW050000160222
22950JS00001B/39